Painting AND Wallpapering

SECRETS

from Brian Santos
The Wall Wizard

WILEY

Wiley Publishing, Inc.

Credits

Acquisitions Editor
Pam Mourouzis

Project Editor
Christina Stambaugh

Copy Editor
Doug Peterson

Vice President and Publisher
Cindy Kitchel

Vice President and Executive Publisher
Kathy Nebenhaus

Page Composition
Erin Zeltner

Cover Design
José Almaguer

Painting and Wallpapering Secrets from Brian Santos The Wall Wizard

Published by Wiley Publishing, Inc., Hoboken, New Jersey
Published simultaneously in Canada

Note to the Readers:
Due to differing conditions, tools and the individual skills, John Wiley & Sons, Inc. assumes no responsibility for any damages, injuries suffered, or losses incurred as a result of following the information published in this book. Before beginning any project, review the instructions carefully, and if any doubts or questions remain, consult local experts or authorities. Because codes and regulations vary greatly, you always should check with authorities to ensure that your project complies with all applicable local codes and regulations. Always read and observe all of the safety precautions provided by manufacturers of any tools, equipment, or supplies, and follow all accepted safety procedures.

For general information on our other products and services or to obtain technical support please contact our Customer Care Department within the U.S. at (877) 762-2974, outside the U.S. at (317) 572-3993 or fax (317) 572-4002.

Wiley also publishes its books in a variety of electronic formats. Some content that appears in print may not be available in electronic books. For more information about Wiley products, please visit our web site at www.wiley.com.

Library of Congress Cataloging-in-Publication Data:
Santos, Brian.
 Painting and wallpapering secrets from Brian Santos, the Wall Wizard / Brian Santos.
  p. cm.
ISBN 978-0-470-59360-8 (pbk)
ISBN 978-0-470-91131-0 (ebk)
 1. House painting—Amateurs' manuals. 2. Paperhanging—Amateurs' manuals. I. Title.
 TT323.S26 2010
 698'.1—dc22

                              2010028548

Printed in the United States of America

10 9 8 7 6 5 4 3 2

Book production by Wiley Publishing, Inc. Composition Services

Dedication

This book is dedicated to YOU!

Within these pages we will explore the mysteries, mistakes, and magic of decorative finishes and reveal that Wall Wizards are made, not born. It took me more than three decades to learn the tricks I share with you in this book. Once you've learned my secrets, don't be afraid to use them. It is my hope that they will serve you well. Every time you apply them, you prove Dorothy was right: There really is *no place like home!*

Thank-Yous

It takes a village to raise a "Wizard." My special thanks:

To my mom, for her artistic influence. To my dad, for his work ethic. To my grandfather, for instilling me with the power of "why."

Thanks to Dan Weeks, who has collaborated with me on this and several other books to bring the voice of the Wizard alive on the page. To Wiley Publishing, Inc., especially Pam Mourouzis and Cindy Kitchel, for their belief in the "magic" of the Wizard.

To my children, Paul, Scott, and Kelli, whom I love, and who are the future.

And most of all, to my wife and partner, Virginia, who shares all my dreams. Thank you for all your love and support throughout our journeys together.

Table of Contents

Meet the Wizard

"That's so cool! How do you do that?" I hear this all the time as I demonstrate painting, faux finishing, and wallpapering techniques in my workshops at home shows around the world. The question that inevitably follows my demonstration is "Can I do that?"

Yes, you can! With an understanding of the materials and techniques involved, almost anyone can create beautiful rooms. And once you know and master some basic principles, the variety of results you can create is virtually limitless.

I'm a fourth-generation decorating contractor. My philosophy is simple: *Knowledge is power*. The real secret to success lies in understanding how to achieve the results you desire. I call this the "why behind the how-to," and it is something most books, classes, and workshops never tell you. How can you know what to do if you don't understand why you're doing it? That's why I wrote this book: to reveal the science behind the magic of decorative finishes and show you how to create some magic of your own.

First we'll talk about how to use and combine color—the foundation of all decorative techniques. We'll discuss what tools and materials you'll need, and how to prepare the room—including my magic wallpaper stripping formula that allows you to strip up to 16 layers of wallpaper at once.

Then we'll explore the techniques themselves: First, paint, the fastest and least expensive way to transform a room. Next, faux finishing, a way to create magical effects using paint, my fail-safe glaze recipe, and simple household tools. Finally, I'll share my "Henry Ford Method" of installing wallpaper. With it, you'll apply wallpaper faster, easier, and with less mess and frustration than many pros.

Along the way, I'll share tips, tricks, and techniques that will make your project go smoothly and take much less time than conventional methods. They're all based on a combination of common sense and professional experience.

My goal in this book is to give you the knowledge and confidence you need to create the home interior you desire—to turn a daunting chore into an exciting opportunity for self expression. When you look at decorating through Wizard eyes, you'll see the magic all around you.

So let's get started!

chapter 1

Color

Your home is your largest, most visible, and most expensive possession. Combining painting, faux finishing, and wallpapering may seem daunting, but the purpose of this book is to help you understand the part that each decorating technique plays in creating the ambiance you're looking for. **Paint** is the foundation of any decorating job. Painting is the most cost effective, accessible way to apply color to your home. **Faux finishing** builds on your painting skills and enables you to apply not just color, but also texture, form, and character to your walls. **Wallpaper** enables you to apply detail to your walls. When used effectively and applied correctly, wallpaper can enhance painting and faux finishing techniques to add drama, impact, and style to your home.

Let's start by talking about color. It's the one element that all three techniques share. Yet few people know the simple rules that govern this important element of design.

First, understand that there is absolutely no wrong color to use. Any color can be livable when the hue, value, intensity, and lighting are correct and in balance. If you want to paint a powder room purple with silver leafing and a black glaze, go for it! These color combinations, used in the appropriate context, scale, and proportion, can be stunning. Used inappropriately, though, they can appear garish and overwhelming.

So go ahead—experiment! If the outcome isn't what you expected, the worst thing that can happen is that you'll have to redo your work—hardly a disaster. In this chapter, I'll explain some common myths, mistakes, and misconceptions about color. You'll learn about proven tools and techniques and be empowered with the knowledge and language of color to express your own style with skill and confidence.

Color BASICS

Effective design depends on the relationship of different colors in a room. Color creates a room's personality, defines its style, sets its mood, controls its space, accents its advantages, and hides its faults. It can turn a dull space into a warm, inviting environment. Yet one color alone can't achieve these benefits. You need a combination of colors that complement and reinforce a particular look or mood. This selection of color combinations becomes your decorating plan.

Changing the wall color and a few accessories creates three different looks in the same room.

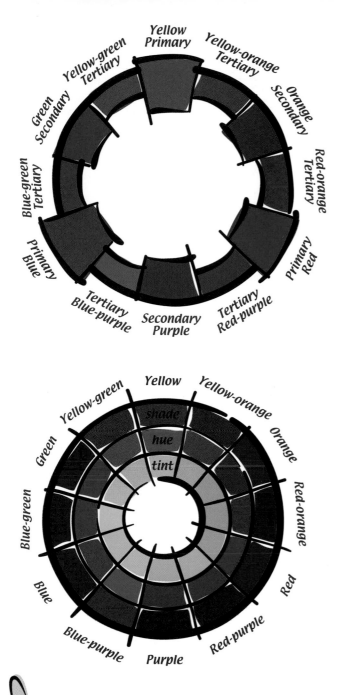

The color wheel

Most people haven't seen a color wheel since middle-school art class or high school home economics, but a Wall Wizard knows it is a handy design tool. A color wheel shows how colors relate to each other. Three relationships are of particular interest: primary, secondary, and tertiary.

PRIMARY COLORS

The most basic of color relationships, primary colors are the three pure colors found in light: red, yellow, and blue. They cannot be broken down into other colors, but when used in various combinations, they create all other colors. Primary colors are equidistant from one another on the color wheel.

SECONDARY COLORS

The second level of colors are orange, green, and purple. Each is created from equal amounts of two primary colors. On the color wheel, each secondary color falls halfway between the two primary colors it contains and directly opposite the third primary color.

TERTIARY COLORS

Tertiary, or third-level, colors are created by combining equal parts of a primary and its adjacent secondary color. Yellow and orange, for example, form yellow-orange.

Color levels build on each other. This means you need primary colors to form secondary colors, and both to develop tertiary colors.

The bottom color wheel presents the differences among pure colors, or hues, shown in the middle ring; shades, created by adding black, shown in the outer ring; and tints, created by adding white, shown in the inner ring.

cool tool

If you can't decide on a color, ask your paint retailer for a color fan deck. This nifty tool shows the exact color combinations a specific manufacturer offers. Use this portable color tool in your home to see how the light in a room influences a particular color. Fan decks at professional paint stores cost about $15 each.

Color VARIATIONS

Mixing basic colors together or with white or black in varying proportions produces thousands of options. All colors have three characteristics: hue, intensity, and value. These variations result in an endless range of colors.

Hue

Hue is the purest form of a color.

Intensity

Intensity describes a color's degree of purity, or saturation. Saturated colors appear more vivid to the eye. You can diminish the intensity of a color by adding either white or black; the color becomes paler or grayer depending on how much you add.

Value

Value refers to the relative lightness or darkness of a color. As a color is mixed with white or black, it moves away from its pure color, becoming a tint or a shade.

- A **tint** is a color that has been lightened by the addition of white. The more white you add, the paler the color. For example, pinks are tints of pure red. On the color wheel, tints lie inside the pure hues and move toward the center of the wheel as they get progressively lighter (page 11).

- A **shade** is a color that has been darkened by the addition of black. The more black you add, the darker the color. Forest green, for example, is a shade of pure green. Shades lie outside the pure colors on the color wheel (page 11) and move outward as they get darker.

The vivid blue above the window combines with the pale green of the walls to display a classic mix of intensities.

Here, all the colors come on strong, from the cabinet fronts to the walls to the border around the mirror.

- A **tone** is a color that has been modified with gray, creating a more subtle version of a color. Mustard is a tone of yellow.

- **Neutral** colors are white, black, and gray, which is a blend of white and black. Technically white and black are noncolors because white reflects all the colors in the full visible spectrum and black absorbs all of them.

Working with different values of various colors in your decorating plan is more pleasing than choosing colors of the same value; it keeps colors from competing against one another. Blue and green, for instance, don't always work well together, but a high-value pastel blue and a low-value dark green can be an effective combination.

Low-value color selections, such as the peach bed ruffle, tablecloth, and pillows, create a quiet atmosphere, perfect for a bedroom.

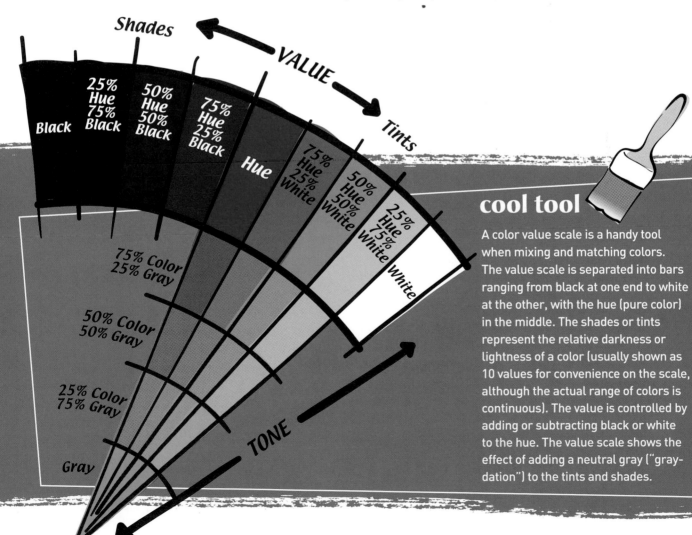

cool tool

A color value scale is a handy tool when mixing and matching colors. The value scale is separated into bars ranging from black at one end to white at the other, with the hue (pure color) in the middle. The shades or tints represent the relative darkness or lightness of a color (usually shown as 10 values for convenience on the scale, although the actual range of colors is continuous). The value is controlled by adding or subtracting black or white to the hue. The value scale shows the effect of adding a neutral gray ("gray-dation") to the tints and shades.

Color COMBINATIONS

The color wheel demystifies color relationships and helps you find colors that work well together. No hard-and-fast rules exist about which colors should be used together, but some natural combinations make successful matches. The following classic combinations are considered the basics for beginners.

Analogous colors

This set uses three colors located next to each other on the color wheel. Analogous colors are harmonious color plans.

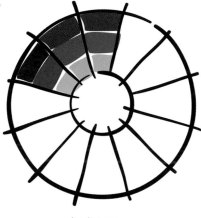

Analogous

Complementary colors

Two colors located opposite each other on the color wheel contrast with and complement each other, creating bold color plans.

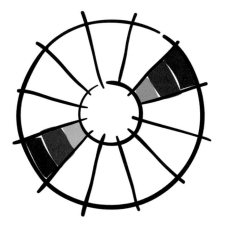

Complementary

Triad colors

Three colors, or a triad, are spaced equidistant from each other on the color wheel, forming complex, lively color plans.

Triad

Monochromatic colors

These schemes use many variations on one color theme to create sophisticated, aesthetic plans.

Color and LIGHT

Light is color; color is light. Color comes to your eyes as reflected light. Change the type of light, and you change the appearance of the color. That's true no matter whether you're talking about paint, wallpaper, carpets, or upholstery—basically anything you put in your home. So you need to control light sources, as well as your paint and wallpaper hues, to control color.

At very least, you need to be aware that the colors you choose will look different depending on the source of light that prevails in the room. Decorating schemes look very different under typical incandescent light than they do in daylight. Fluorescent tube lighting comes in several colors, all of which contribute their own colorcast.

Natural light is sunlight, the purest light and the easiest on the eye. It covers the entire spectrum of light and shows the truest color.

General lighting is also known as ambient lighting. This artificial light can come from incandescent, fluorescent, halogen, or LED sources. "Daylight" bulbs—available in fluorescent, compact fluorescent, and LED versions—provide a broader spectrum of light than standard bulbs and produce a more natural effect, so your room's colors don't change when the sun goes down and the lights are switched on.

Task lighting highlights a workspace or feature area. Track lighting and under-cabinet lighting are examples of this type of light.

Accent or specialty lighting adds visual interest and drama to your decor. Lamps are common examples of accent lighting.

quiz the WIZ

Why does the paint look different on the wall than it did on the sample card?

You probably selected the color by looking at it under a different type or intensity of light than what's in your room. Sunlight, daylight, fluorescent light, halogen light, and incandescent light affect colors differently. So bring the sample into the room you intend to decorate and look at it several times during the day. See how the color looks using different kinds of artificial light before making a final decision. To get an even better idea of how the color will look in your room, purchase a small quantity of the paint and apply it to a white foam core board, then view the board in several positions in the room you plan to decorate. Place the sample board directly on the surface you intend to decorate, as apparent color changes with the angle at which the material is placed relative to the light source.

Decorating PYRAMID

Many people who attend my color workshops ask: Where do I start decorating? My answer is to plan in one direction and work in the opposite direction. Let me explain:

This pyramid illustrates how to create a decorating plan. Start your planning with the least changeable design element in a room and work toward the easiest to change. So rather than starting with the walls, which can be painted a different color every week, build your decorating project literally from the ground up. Consider first the carpet or floor covering. Then move up to the drapes and upholstery, based on your flooring choice. Continue up the pyramid until you reach paint, the crowning glory of the room.

With your plan complete, it's time to get to work. Start with paint and work your way through the other design elements in the room.

PAINT

When all other design elements are present, choose the appropriate color to paint the walls.

ACCESSORIES

Accessories, such as collectibles and displays, add personality and style to a room.

LIGHTING

Some lighting is permanent or fixed; lamp lighting and under-counter lighting can highlight areas and add dimension. Lighting also sets the mood in a room.

ARTWORK

Artwork reflects a sense of style and adds personality to a room.

FURNITURE

Furniture is expensive to replace, but rearranging pieces can completely change a room's look. The style of furniture creates a particular atmosphere.

FABRIC

Coordinate fabric for upholstery and drapes with flooring. Fabrics with a design and pattern give you a built-in selection of dominant and accent colors.

FLOORING

Choose carpeting, wood, vinyl, or linoleum floors first. These big-ticket items are expensive and time-consuming to change. A neutral shade gives you the most flexibility in your design plan, whereas a pattern or colorful floor can enliven a room.

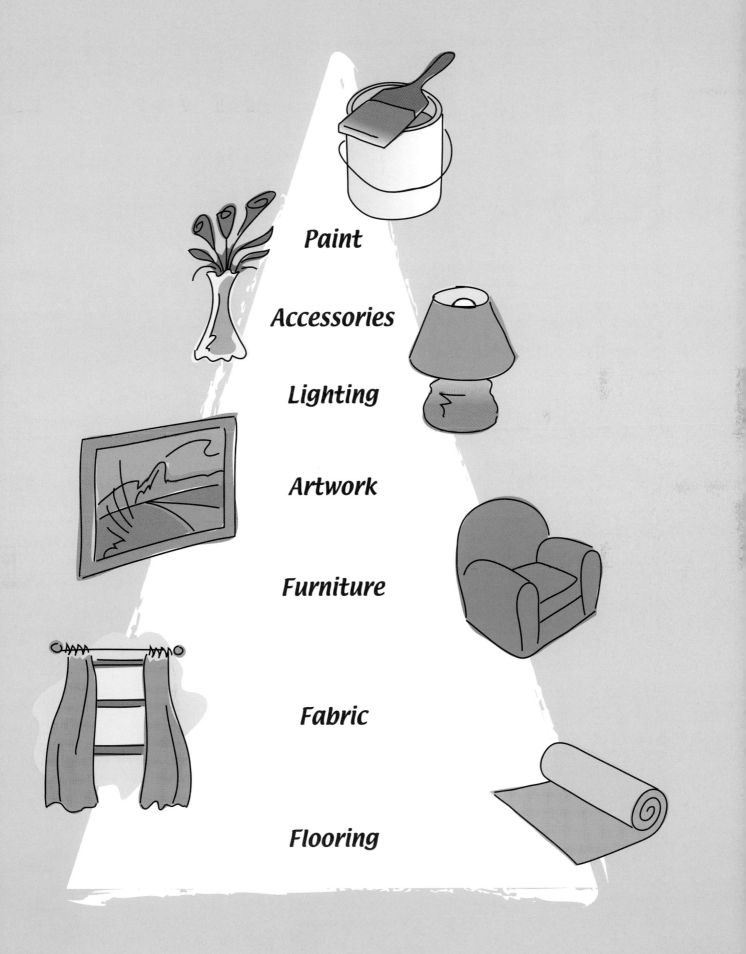

Paint

Accessories

Lighting

Artwork

Furniture

Fabric

Flooring

quiz the WIZ

How can I choose color like a Wall Wizard?

Here are several techniques to help you on your color quest:

- For white walls throughout the house, use the same value of white in every room for a unifying effect.

- Use differences of scale and proportion to create interest in a room. Using all pale tints in a room can make the colors look weak and dull, using only mid-tones produces monotony, and a plan composed entirely of dark shades will feel gloomy. Combinations, however, create a dynamic and refreshing décor.

- If you choose different colors for different rooms, decorate spaces between the rooms, such as foyers, hallways, and staircases, in grayed-down colors to create transitions.

- Pick a color for your home and use it in different amounts in each room. It can be the dominant color in one room, the secondary color in another, an accent color in the third, and the color of an accessory in a fourth, for example. This technique will create harmony throughout the house.

The combination of color tones in this bedroom creates a dynamic and refreshing space.

Pastel hues add to the light, expansive feel of this room.

Stopping the wall color below the ceiling lowers the visual height of the room, making it feel cozier.

The dark colors here make the room more intimate. The monochromatic plan uses a variety of textures to add interest.

- Light colors are expansive and airy; they make rooms seem larger and brighter. Dark colors are sophisticated and warm; they make large rooms feel more intimate.

- If you want dark or intensely colored walls, tint the primer the same color as the finish coat.

- Camouflage architectural defects by using neutral colors that blend with neutral walls, ceilings, and floors.

- Carry the wall color up to the ceiling to raise the visual height of a room. If there is a crown or cove molding, paint it the same color. A light color also makes the ceiling seem higher.

- To lower a ceiling or make a room feel cozy, stop the wall color 9 to 12 inches below the ceiling. You can also paint the ceiling a dark color.

- Make a long, narrow room seem wider by coloring the shorter walls darker than the longer walls.

- To coordinate a room, slightly tint white ceiling paint by adding a splash of the wall color.

Why can't my spouse and I agree on color selections?

It's an age-old question with an age-old answer: Men and women see colors differently. Women have more cones (light-sensitive receptor cells) in their eyes, making them more able to distinguish among the slightest variations in colors. Men, on the other hand, have more rods (a different type of receptor cells) in their eyes, making them more responsive to motion but less attuned to color.

PICKING a Wall Color

Walls are the largest surfaces in a room, and how you finish them affects every other aspect of your decorating plan. Here are three methods you can use to choose a wall color:

Choose it first

If the walls are the most important feature in the room, choose their finish first and then build your decorating plan around them. Why not indulge yourself and choose one of your favorite colors? Or decide what mood you want a room to convey and pick your color accordingly.

Choose it last

If walls will form the backdrop, choose their color after selecting the room's other major elements. Then pull a coordinating color from one of those sources. Choosing a new finish for the walls this way works best when you're not planning to change anything else in the room.

Choose a neutral color

Use a neutral color on the walls, making them a backdrop for other elements in the room, such as its architecture, furnishings, or art.

Just choose!

Taping color samples on the wall doesn't get the job done. You can't swim without first diving in, and you can't decorate without making some choices. So go ahead—take the plunge! Even if you decide you don't like your choices, you can redo. After all, artists frequently change their works before creating a masterpiece. And even professional decorators change their minds as they work through their jobs. The tips and tricks I share in this book are a result of my 25 years of trial and error. They're designed to empower you, not intimidate you. So go ahead, make a choice and get started—you'll find it rewarding and empowering.

In some cases, walls serve as background for other major elements that demand attention, such as a painting.

Furnishings take center stage here, while the walls, painted a neutral color, serve only as a backdrop.

The wall color sets the mood for energetic entertaining in this room; the other elements follow.

Controlling SPACE with Color

Besides being an important design element, the color on your walls has the ability to manipulate your perception of a room. Here are some tricks for using wall and trim colors to achieve various effects:

To make a room appear more spacious, use light colors, subtle textures, and small patterns. To visually raise a low ceiling, consider a strong vertical pattern.

To make a room seem cozier and more intimate, use dark or intense colors; bold, coarse textures; and large patterns.

Painting the pillar the same color as the walls minimizes its impact on this room setting.

To highlight architectural features such as woodwork, moldings, fireplaces, doors, and windows, paint them a color that contrasts with the walls to make them stand out.

To streamline a room's design, paint moldings and other features the same color as the walls to diminish their presence.

Combining techniques to create décor

Paint, faux finishing, and wallpapering all have their place in the decorating process.

Paint enables you to quickly, easily, and inexpensively cover large expanses of wall with just about any color you can imagine. Painted walls create the canvas on which the drama of a room's composition plays out.

Faux finishing builds on your basic painting skills, enabling you to create focal point walls and other elements that add depth, texture, and custom character to your room.

Wallpapering involves a different skill set and enables you to add a richness of material, pattern, and detail that complements paint and faux finishing.

I encourage you to think first about painted surfaces. While paint is often not the first element we select, it's the first thing that we apply, and it binds together all the other elements. That's why we'll discuss painting first, then faux finishing, and, finally, wallpapering. But first, we'll take a look at all the cool tools you'll use to make your decorating jobs easier—and the preparation that will ensure your project's success.

wizard WARNING

Wall Wizards like a change of scenery, but as a beginning decorator, you should build your skills by applying colors in a private area of your home—a bedroom, bathroom, or laundry room, for example. Even a storage room or garage is a good place to experiment. When you've mastered these spaces, it's much easier to produce professional results in the more visible rooms in your home.

chapter 2

Tools

You don't need to spend a lot of money to be a successful decorator, but you do need the right equipment. You'll find a lot of choices in tools. I've tried about every tool available and even invented a few of my own. In the process, I've found that the best tools meet four simple criteria:

- **They're good quality.** Quality wears better, lasts longer, and produces better results. I've been using many of my painting tools daily for decades, and they're still going strong. If you buy quality, you don't have to keep replacing cheap, broken, worn-out tools or risk having them fail in the middle of a job.

- **They're made of stainless steel or plastic.** These materials are unaffected by paints, strippers, pastes, and solvents. Because they don't rust, they don't contaminate the materials you're working with. Plus, they're easy to clean and long-lasting. For storing paints, wallpaper stripping, and cleaning solutions, nothing beats unbreakable, sealable plastic containers with airtight lids.

- **They're brightly colored.** Fluorescent green, yellow, and orange tools are easy to spot in a work area.

- **They're ergonomic.** Big, comfortable grips promote better tool control and reduce muscle fatigue and the risk of repetitive-strain injuries such as carpal tunnel syndrome. Easy, stress-free work yields better results.

In this chapter, I'll share with you my favorite tools, based on decades of daily use. Some are old standbys, others are newly developed, and still others are tools you can make yourself from inexpensive, readily available materials—or common household products you can repurpose to make your decorating jobs easier. Specialty tools needed for faux finishing projects are covered in chapter 5, "Faux Finishing."

I'll also save you the frustration of bringing the wrong tool to the job by sharing with you some good versus bad tool choices in a variety of categories.

SOLVENTS

Solvents dissolve other materials. They are described as cold, warm, or hot according to their degree of volatility, chemical makeup, and use.

Cold. Fabric softener mixed with water dissolves water-based paints. Water-based cleaning products, such as trisodium phosphate (TSP), ammonia, hydrogen peroxide, and all-purpose cleaners, remove dirt and are neutralized with distilled white vinegar. These products are people-safe and earth-friendly.

Warm. Denatured alcohol, acetone, muriatic acid, and rubbing alcohol can dissolve water or oil solutions and are effective surface cleaners if rinsed off well. They are safe when handled, stored, and disposed of properly.

Hot. Mineral spirits and paint thinners, naphtha, turpentine, and lacquer thinner are hot solvents formulated to break down the chemistry of oil-based paints. Be sure to protect yourself and handle these materials with caution. Use, store, and dispose of these hazardous materials properly.

cool tool

One of my inventions, a bucket trolley allows you to keep a bucket of primer, sealer, or fresh water for cleaning close at hand. Buy a large, round plastic planter base with casters and a length of 2-inch foam pipe insulation from a garden store or home center. Wrap the pipe insulation around the lip of the planter base for a bumper, and you have a bucket trolley that you can roll around the room with a gentle nudge of your toe when your hands are full of tools or other materials.

CLEANING Tools

Have these tools on hand before you start your project:

Keep various sizes of **plastic trash bags** and **resealable plastic bags** handy for storing hardware and switch plates. For dusty cleanup tasks, a **shop vacuum cleaner,** a **push broom** with dustpan, and a **dusting brush** will come in handy. You'll need **5-gallon buckets,** clean-rinsing **tile sponges,** a **sponge-head floor mop with nylon scrubbing pads,** and a **nylon-bristle deck brush** with extension pole. Large **household sponges** with a nylon scrubbing pad, **2-quart plastic buckets,** and lots of **terrycloth towels** will round out your cleaning supplies.

wizard WARNING

Have a cleanup bucket ready at the start of any decorating project. Why? Because the moment you open a container of paint, glaze, or wallpaper adhesive, you risk spilling it. Fill a 5-gallon bucket about two-thirds full of water and place a tile sponge in it. (If you like, you can use a smaller bucket for greater mobility.) Place this bucket in the middle of the room with a large towel beneath it. Use a damp sponge to absorb and clean up any spills; a rag will smear and spread the mess. Change the water often. Have plenty of shop rags or towels around to soak up water spills. Keep several other 5-gallon buckets with lids around for cleaning tools and mixing and storing paint.

Protect yourself

Start with the most important tool: you. Never come into contact with paints, stains, solvents, or adhesives. Why? Because your body is a giant sponge, and you can absorb these chemicals through your skin. To protect yourself, wear nonporous **vinyl gloves.** Latex gloves tear easily and are porous, allowing liquids to seep through. Sprinkle **baby powder** into the gloves so they slip on easily. Wrap a piece of masking tape around each cuff to seal it. To protect bare arms, spray on some **nonstick cooking oil;** it will prevent water-based paint from penetrating your skin. I figure if you can eat it, you can wear it!

For full-body protection, put on **disposable paper coveralls** and a **painter's hat** or **shower cap.** Wear **goggles,** safety glasses, or a face shield to protect your eyes from dust, chips, or paint. A **dust mask** filters out dust, and a **respirator** protects you from dust and chemical fumes.

wizard WARNING

Use plastic wrap as a fast, easy way to cover doorknobs and to keep speckles and splatters off hardware and phones. Press a sheet of plastic wrap over your eyeglasses too. You can still see through them, but the wrap protects the lenses from paint drops.

cool tool

Anything you don't want to get liquids on, including yourself, should be covered. Here's a work apron that's inexpensive, easy to make, and keeps you clean. Lay out a 13-gallon tall kitchen plastic trash bag (a trash compactor bag works best) with the sealed end at the top and the open end down. Fold it in half lengthwise. Opposite the folded edge, use scissors to cut off the top corner in an arcing cut to make the armholes (first cut). Make the second cut to create the neck straps, starting about 1 inch below the sealed top edge, cutting parallel about 1 inch in from the first cut. The third cut forms the waist ties. Tie the neck straps together. Save the pouches created by the first cut; you can use them to store a paint can lid.

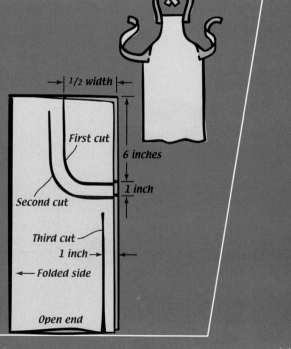

1/2 width

First cut

6 inches

1 inch

Second cut

Third cut

1 inch

Folded side

Open end

Protect the room

Everyone thinks of 2-inch-wide masking tape when it's time for painting. But that beige-colored tape has adhesive that is so sticky, it can sometimes rip the paint and wallpaper right off your woodwork and walls. One of the best things to happen for painters is the development of different types of **masking tapes** designed to perform best with various types of paint. **Blue tape** is designed for latex paints and other water-based finishes. **Purple tape** is for oil-based finishes. **Green tape** is for lacquers. All three stay on regardless of humidity and stick for at least seven days. But the real benefit of these new colored masking tapes is that they pull off any surface—even paint or wallpaper—without causing damage. Colored tape is an insurance policy that protects you from messy mistakes.

Pretaped **masking film** has a built-in cutter and is designed to easily dispense a replaceable roll of masking tape and plastic sheeting. The film unfolds to about 24 inches, providing a drop cloth that protects surrounding surfaces from spills and splatters. The film clings to a surface so it won't flip up into a freshly painted surface, and it is biodegradable, so you can throw it away with the trash. You can use **lip balm** to mask glass panes when painting window trim to allow for easy glass cleanup.

Why invest in a big, heavy tarp like the pros use when you'll only use it five times in your life? Instead, purchase a **disposable paper/plastic drop cloth.** Face the paper side up to absorb and the plastic side down to protect a surface. This product is nonslip so you won't go sliding across it, and it is biodegradable, so you can wad it up and toss it in the trash when you are finished.

For protecting furniture and other items that are too big to move, use **9×12-foot, 0.7-mil plastic sheeting** because it provides a lot of coverage. It is inexpensive and biodegradable, so you can throw it away when you're finished. It does have one drawback: It is hard to unfold. Here's a trick: Take the plastic, still in the package, and place it in the freezer for about 30 minutes. This removes the static charge on the plastic, so when you take it out, it's easy to unfold. If you immediately lay it out over furniture, it will wrap itself around the furniture as it warms up. One more tip: Don't use old bedsheets or newspapers when you paint. The paint will go right through them, staining the surface beneath.

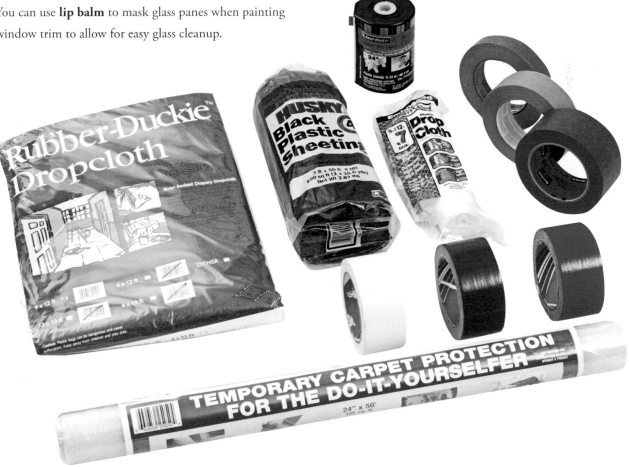

Sanding

A variety of **sandpaper sheets** with grits from 60 to 400 are necessary to properly sand surfaces. A **sanding block** to smooth a patching job, along with a **palm sander** or half-sheet orbital sander, works nicely as well. A pivoting **drywall sander** uses a nonclogging abrasive screen rather than sandpaper, and it has an extension pole for high or hard-to-reach places. Some pole sanders can be hooked to a shop vacuum, which sucks up the dust before it can escape into the air. If heavy sanding is required, wear a particle **dust mask** and place a **box fan** in a window to blow the dust out. Never use wet tools to remove dust; the water will turn the dust to mud and coat the surface. A sticky **tack rag** picks up fine dust between coats of paint. **Tile sponges** and **nylon scrubbing pads** are used for wet sanding.

Wallpaper removal

Removing wallpaper requires a few tools. Use a **broom handle** to roll strippable wallpaper off the wall. A **rolling mop bucket** eliminates the need to repeatedly bend over and move it (or use a bucket trolley, page 24). A 3-gallon plastic **pump sprayer** quickly applies wallpaper remover to large areas; use a **trigger-handle spray bottle** for smaller areas. Buy a new sprayer; don't use one that has been used for herbicides or pesticides. A **Paper Tiger** is a handy tool that perforates wallpaper and makes it easier to remove. A **paper scraper** has a wide, flat edge that is angled so it easily lifts wallpaper from the surface. Never substitute a broad knife for a paper scraper.

You will also need **baking soda, fabric softener,** and **wallpaper remover concentrate** with enzymes to make the potion for wallpaper removal. Stir 1 cup of **vinegar** into 1 gallon of water to rinse walls. Have several clean **5-gallon buckets** on hand. Have plenty of **0.7-mil plastic sheeting** to cover the walls from top to bottom.

Wall repair

You will need **fiberglass mesh reinforcing tape** and **quick-drying plaster compound** for medium-size holes. For large holes, have a **drywall saw,** scraps of drywall, paper joint tape, oil-based sealer, and **wallboard screws** on hand. To drive the fasteners, you'll want a corded or cordless **drill driver** (cordless models are more convenient). You'll also need a **tape measure,** a **utility knife,** and a **drywall square** or **carpenter's square** to measure and cut the drywall.

Filling materials include all-purpose joint compound, plaster patching, and quickset patching mud. For convenience in mixing large buckets of joint compound, chuck a **mixing auger** into your drill. Several sizes of **taping knives** smooth the drywall compound after your patch is applied. Carry material in a mudding tray. **Slotted-head** and **Phillips screwdrivers** come in handy for opening containers and snugging down drywall screws; a **hammer** and **ring-shank drywall nails** are used to hang sheets.

painting from the pantry

Here's a $2 Wall Wizard solution for cleanup: baby wipes. Think about it: These wipes are designed to clean up really big messes. The alcohol in the wipes removes any grease, grime, and dirt; the lanolin renders them nonflammable. They're biodegradable, plus they smell better than dirty old rags.

PAINTING Tools

Extend your reach

The **multiladder** is a sturdy, lightweight, and practical home improvement tool. One handy size grows to 16 feet long when fully extended and is composed of four 4-foot-long sections with multiposition locking hinges between each section. It can be configured as an extension ladder or as a stepladder. You can also create a level work platform on uneven surfaces, such as a stairway or ramp. And here's a great **Wizard Trick:** Configure the middle two sections horizontally and the end sections down for legs. Place a sheet of plywood on top of the multiladder and you have a work table.

If you have a high ceiling or stairwell, you might need **scaffolding.** You can rent scaffolding from most equipment rental outlets. The easiest type to use has locking wheels and folds for transport or storage. Look for scaffolding that is narrow enough to roll through a standard doorway.

A lightweight **2-step platform ladder** is my choice for giving you a step up in the world. Its sturdy yet simple design allows you to face the wall while you work. It weighs only 10 pounds, so you can easily close it with one hand by lifting up the built-in shelf, and it also folds 3 inches flat for storage. When opened it has two steps: The upper one is a 12- to 18-inch platform, which is easier to stand on than a standard ladder rung and brings you comfortably within reach of an 8-foot ceiling. The ladder has a built-in safety cage, and it is wide enough to bridge over a toilet but narrow enough to place into a bathtub.

tips 'n' tricks

Add peel-and-stick traction strips, available at most hardware stores and home centers, to each step of the platform ladder to keep your feet from sliding. (You can put the same strips on the steps of a multiladder, too.) Put white rubber cane tips, available from hardware stores and pharmacies, on the bottoms of the legs for better stability and so the ladder won't scuff or scratch surfaces, such as floors or bathtubs.

Paintbrushes

Paintbrushes are the most basic of painting tools. They spread paint efficiently and are easy to control. If you care for them properly, paintbrushes can last for years. Both of my brushes are more than 15 years old, and except for a paint fleck here or there, they look brand new. To choose your own brush:

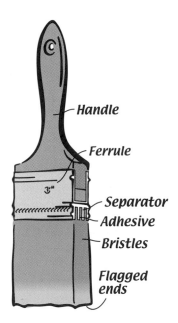

Handle
Ferrule
Separator
Adhesive
Bristles
Flagged ends

- **Look for a brush with a sturdy hardwood handle,** an aluminum or stainless-steel ferrule (the band that covers the joint where the bristles meet the handle) and bristles tapered at their ends so they form an even line when pressed against a flat surface.

- **Grip the brush by the handle;** the handle should rest comfortably in your palm, fingers on one side of the ferrule, thumb on the other.

- **Fan out the bristles.** Look for flagging: split ends on the bristles. More flagging in the bristles means that a brush will lay paint on the surface better.

- **Flex the bristles.** They should feel springy, not limp or stiff.

- **Use the correct brush for your chosen paint.** If you apply paint with the wrong type of brush, the paint will not flow correctly. For oil-based paints, purchase a china-bristle brush. These are natural boar's hair brushes that do not absorb oil but allow it to flow in an even, controlled manner. They are generally black and warm to the touch. For water-based paints, purchase a synthetic/nylon-bristle brush. Water-based paint won't stick to nylon bristles. Nylon bristles are usually beige or cream-colored and cool to the touch.

This nylon-bristle sash brush is ideal for painting window muntins, sashes, and moldings.

This nylon-bristle brush is designed for cutting-in and trim work with latex paints.

This china-bristle trim brush is angled to help you paint a clean, sharp line when cutting in edges with oil-based paints.

This 4-inch brush holds lots of paint and applies it in a broad swath. It's good for painting large surfaces.

cool tool

Take the "pain" out of painting. To avoid carpal tunnel syndrome, blisters, and cramps, make a soft grip for your paintbrush. Take 2-inch diameter pipe insulation, trim to the right length, and shove it over the handle of your paintbrush.

cool tools

The right tools make a project go easier, faster, and safer. Here are a few basics for painting:

- **A 10-in-1 paint can opener is the proper tool for opening a paint can.** You can also use it to punch holes in the rim of the can so paint will run inside instead of outside the can and for resealing the lid without damage.

- Two or three coats of **rubber cement** keep paint off door hinges and barrels.

- **The basic tool to deliver and manage paint as you apply it to a surface is a 2-quart plastic bucket.** This size bucket is also handy to mix a paint color and to use in cleaning up. For rolling, look for a plastic, square paint bucket with a built-in paint grid. It's a faster, neater way to load your roller evenly. You also can buy a separate paint grid to hang in your own bucket (get plastic rather than metal). Another tip: I line my bucket with a heavy-duty plastic trash compactor bag, secured to the rim with a small bungee cord. I can twist-tie off the top if I need to pause while painting, and when I'm finished painting, I just throw out the empty bag.

- **If you're going to use a conventional roller tray,** get a heavy-gauge metal one; it won't bend when you pick it up the way a plastic tray might. But what about rust and paint contamination? Never pour paint directly into a metal tray. Use a plastic disposable liner or a plastic bag as a liner. You'll save on cleanup time too.

- **Dish soap bottles make great paint and glaze delivery containers.** Clear plastic lets you see the color. They're easy to grip and squeeze to deliver the contents. The nozzle allows you to dispense the amount you need, then seal the bottle airtight.

- A **plastic paint shield** protects a surface while you paint an adjoining wall or ceiling.

- **When painting, use a box fan to prevent fumes from building up.** In a room without ventilation, put the fan in the doorway on the floor to blow fresh air into the bottom of the room, forcing contaminated air up and out the top of the doorway. For rooms with windows, put the fan in a window blowing outward. Open another window or a door (ideally as far from the fan as possible) to create a fresh airflow through the room.

Paint rollers

You'll be tempted to buy a cheap, throw-away fuzzy-napped roller, but save yourself the headache! A **9½-inch foam paint roller** works faster, easier, and better. You can load three or four times the amount of paint onto the roller. Such porosity means less dipping into the roller tray, which means more coverage in less time. Another advantage is that a foam pad will roll over any surface—textured, lap siding, stucco—because it is designed to conform to any surface it touches. A foam roller won't splatter paint or leave fuzzies in the paint on the wall. If you purchase a roller with a nylon core, it is easier to clean, and you can use it over and over. Yellow foam covers are designed for applying water-based paint. Gray or blue foam covers are for oil-based paint.

When selecting a roller frame, choose heavy-duty plastic or stainless steel. Make sure the handle is comfortable to grip and has a threaded socket in the end so you can add an extension pole. Or buy a frame with a telescoping handle. My favorite has a handle that can expand from 12 to 32 inches, making it easy to roll the wall from floor to ceiling. If using an extension pole, a 4-foot extension pole works best; it's long enough to help you paint from floor to ceiling, yet short enough to work in a closet. Get a fiberglass handle, not an aluminum one. Fiberglass will not conduct electricity, so if you should happen to make contact with a live outlet or fixture, you won't get hurt. Fiberglass also bends slightly, giving you better feedback on how much pressure you're putting on the roller.

Mini rollers—sometimes called "hot-dog rollers" because of their shape—are great. These 4-inch-wide rollers make it easy to paint small surfaces or in constrained spaces, and they apply paint as evenly as the larger

versions. Plus they paint into corners, so you don't need to cut in these areas with a brush. Corner rollers, which are narrow and tapered to an edge, are also ideal for getting into tight corners. The beveled shape and foam material is designed to evenly roll paint on both surfaces of an inside corner.

Paint pads

The **4-inch paint pad** has a lot to offer. It's made of plastic, with a short, thick ergonomic handle. Tracking wheels set off the application pad from adjacent moldings. The bristle face of a pad is perfect for cutting in, edging, and painting flat trim. The pad's foam core holds three times more paint than a brush, has five times more surface area than a regular brush tip, and has bristles that are only ¼ inch long, so the paint won't dry out. It splatters and drips less than a brush. Most pads even come with a plastic paint tray and airtight snap-on lid.

cool tools

What good is a tool if it's not with you? That's the logic behind making a painter's tool belt.

- **Belt.** Begin with a 2-inch snap-buckle nylon web belt, available from home centers and hardware stores.

- **Rag holder.** Cut the top off a 1-liter plastic soda bottle at an angle to make a holder for rags or a package of baby wipes. Cut two slits in the back so it will slide onto the belt. This handy container prevents your clothing and skin from coming into contact with chemicals that seep from the rags.

- **Dusting brush and magnetic holder.** Cut the handle off a 4-inch polyester/nylon paintbrush with a stainless steel ferrule. To hold the brush to the belt, use a 2-inch round pot magnet, so named because it was designed to hold brushes to the side of a metal paint pot. Cover the magnet with duct tape to keep it from scratching the tool. Then fasten the magnet to the belt with a machine bolt, nylon locknut, and two fender washers.

- **10-in-1 tool and line.** Bolt a retractable lingerie clothesline to the belt and tie your 10-in-1 or other tool to the line. Attach another pot magnet next to the reel to hold the tool when it's not in use. (Secure another pot magnet to the belt for holding other metal tools. The magnet is strong enough to hold a small hammer or screwdriver.)

- **Hook-and-loop hanger.** Apply the hook side of a piece of self-adhesive hook-and-loop tape to the belt. Attach the loop side to any other tools you want to keep on your belt.

- **Tool holder.** Make it the same as the rag holder for extra tools, such as a dish soap loading bottle, hand tools, or prep materials.

- If the belt seems too heavy to wear around your waist, add suspenders for support. If you want to, you can hang more tools on the suspenders.

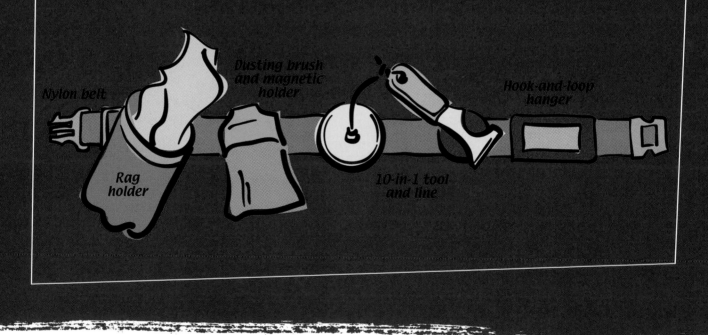

Nylon belt

Dusting brush and magnetic holder

Rag holder

10-in-1 tool and line

Hook-and-loop hanger

cool tools

Leave that ladder behind! You can work a room floor to ceiling and never have to climb a step—with make-'em-yourself bucket stilts.

I am vertically challenged, so I created bucket stilts to make it easy to reach the top of walls and trim. Buy two 5-gallon paint buckets with lids. Trace your shoe outline on the lid and mark the attachment points at the toe and heel. Attach double-sided hook-and-loop straps to the lids with machine bolts, fender washers, and nylon locknuts. Secure the two shorter straps across the toes and the two longer straps at the heel to wrap around your ankles. Glue a large rubber pad to the bottom of each bucket to prevent slipping. Snap the lids onto each bucket, stand on the lids, and strap in. Now you are a full 18 inches taller than before and fully mobile. You can store painting tools in the empty buckets when not in use.

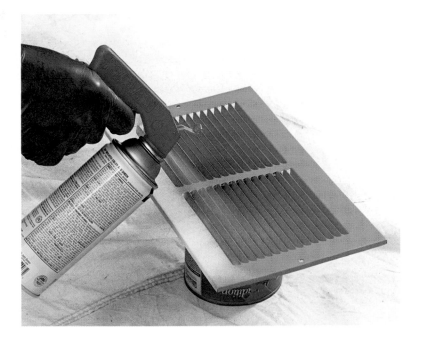

Sprayers and power rollers

If your job calls for a small amount of painting, or if you need even coverage on an irregular surface, spray painting is hard to beat.

SPRAY CANS

Spray cans produce a fine, smooth surface if used carefully. A snap-on spray-can handle grip gives you better control when using a spray can. The handle grip also protects the nozzle from being snapped off inside the pressure valve, a common problem that renders the can and its contents useless.

POWER SPRAYERS

Sprayers are great for covering large surfaces, but they tend to use more paint than a brush or roller. They work well on irregular surfaces, such as louvered doors, panels, and wrought-iron trim. Inexpensive consumer models make sense if you need to spray just a few items and if you are patient. Follow carefully the directions for preparing and applying the paint and for cleaning.

The best spray tool for interior painting is a high-volume, low-pressure (HVLP) paint sprayer. More expensive than a typical consumer-model sprayer, it produces less overspray and a finer finish. An HVLP sprayer can also handle almost any kind of paint and is much less finicky about paint viscosity, or "runniness," so it is less likely to clog. Preparations and masking are especially important when spray painting because everything that is not sealed or covered will end up with an overspray of paint.

POWER ROLLERS

Here's some advice from someone who has tried all the gimmicks and gadgets on the market: If you're the type who jumps right into a project, don't invest in power rollers and sprayers. It takes practice to learn how to use them properly. By the time you figure out how to put it together, fidget with viscosity flow, and fumble your way through cleanup, you could have finished the paint job with a brush or manual roller.

If you do find yourself attracted to power painting equipment, practice your technique on low-key projects before tackling high-visibility jobs. Try spraying shutters before kitchen cabinets or rolling the garage walls before painting your living room.

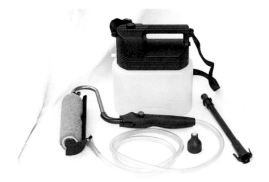

A high-volume, low-pressure (HVLP) paint sprayer is a great tool for interior painting. It spreads an even coat of paint on irregular surfaces, such as louvered doors or trim.

Basic WALLPAPERING Tools

Tool pouch

A large leather pouch holds tools as you work. Leather is soft and flexible, so it doesn't impede mobility, yet it's tough enough to allow you to snap off snap-blade knife tips inside the pouch, which then safely contains the tips. The pouch has a belt of nylon webbing that's lightweight, comfortable, and easy to put on and take off with a quick-release buckle.

Wallpaper smoothing brush

This is the oldest and most indispensable wallpaper application tool. Buy a 12-inch-long bright-colored plastic one that's easy to find and clean. With two passes it can cover the width of a sheet of wallpaper, allowing you to work quickly. The bristles act like hundreds of little fingers that massage the air from beneath the paper, creating a vacuum that holds the covering to the wall until the adhesive starts to set. The bristles apply pressure evenly so they don't damage the material or stretch it out of shape. You can also tamp a seam into place with the bristles before you smooth it down.

Trimming guards

A 4-inch broad knife fits in your tool pouch. Use it to gently hold the wallpaper securely against the wall so it doesn't move when you trim away the waste. Its metal blade protects the wallpaper underneath from knife slips yet is small enough to work around irregular surfaces accurately. The 12- and 24-inch guards have long, straight stainless-steel blades that are used as straightedge guides for ensuring that you make a perfectly straight cut when cutting borders and double-cutting seams.

Chalkline

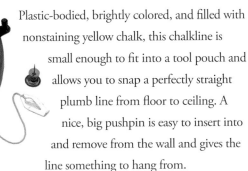

Plastic-bodied, brightly colored, and filled with nonstaining yellow chalk, this chalkline is small enough to fit into a tool pouch and allows you to snap a perfectly straight plumb line from floor to ceiling. A nice, big pushpin is easy to insert into and remove from the wall and gives the line something to hang from.

Float

A wallpaper float fits comfortably in your hand. Use it to set seams with light up-and-down strokes. You can also use a float to gently remove bubbles from beneath wallpaper while the adhesive is still wet by pulling it slowly toward you over the bubble. Never push the tool forward because it can plow or gouge into the surface.

Laser level

This high-tech alternative to the plumb line and chalkline throws a perfectly straight, unwavering beam of colored light over a considerable distance and eliminates the need to climb a ladder and stick a pushpin in the wall. It's a timesaver when working on particularly large or tall surfaces, such as in stairwells or rooms with cathedral ceilings. It also allows you to create a perfectly horizontal line—making it a great tool to have when installing borders—without the chalk residue.

WALLPAPERING: Task-Grouped Tools

Wallpaper application is a multistep process, so you will use different tools at different stages. Here they are grouped by project stage. As you begin each operation, refer to this page to see which tools to gather.

Layout tools

These tools are used to create the layout, the first step in any wallpapering job. You'll use a **tape measure** for measuring the room, a **pencil** for marking your layout on the walls, and a **notepad** for recording the number and length of each sheet.

Processing tools

You'll use this group of tools to process the wallpaper—to precut and label the sheets before activating the adhesive and applying them to the wall. **Framing squares** are used as cutting guides to make perfectly square, straight cuts, both when slicing through the material with a **snap-blade knife** and when tearing the material directly against the square's edge. **Aluminum squares** don't rust and are light and easy to handle; **steel squares** are heavier and handy for keeping materials that tend to curl flat on your layout table. **Scissors** offer an alternative method for cutting wallpaper; **cutting guides** are great for cutting angled sheets for stairwells or slanted ceilings. **Rubber bands** secure back-rolled materials in their rolled form. **Spring clamps** are useful anytime you need an extra hand, such as when applying adhesive to borders. Fasten clamps to the table with **duct tape.**

Pasting tools

An **activation tray** facilitates activation of the adhesive on prepasted wallpaper. I use a flower box—it's made of tough ABS plastic that won't split, crack, or shatter and holds 3½ gallons of water. Nonpasted wallpaper requires a **paint roller** and either a foam- or fiber-nap **roller cover,** a **paint roller tray,** and **adhesive.** A **border applicator** applies adhesive to borders and comes preloaded with adhesive. Kitchen- or trash-compactor-size plastic **trash bags** prevent the pasted or activated wallpaper from drying out while they're being transported and are waiting to be applied to the wall; the bags are used for job cleanup later. An **oversize indelible marker** marks the trash bags—not the wallpaper sheets themselves—with the numbers of the sheets inside.

Installation tools

A **tool pouch** keeps tools at hand while you work, saving time and energy. A **slider pouch** holds **snap-blade knives** for trimming wallpaper sheets after they've been applied to the wall. The larger pouch holds additional knives, boxes of **knife blade refills,** a **wallpaper smoothing brush** for applying wallpaper to the wall, a **4-inch broad knife,** and a **plastic float.** The large pouch also provides a safe place to snap off used blade tips and contain them until they can be discarded safely. The total cost of these tools is less than that of a cordless drill; but with the exception of the expendable knife blades, they'll last you a lifetime.

Tools: GOOD and BAD

I've found that there are good tools and bad tools and that sometimes having the right tool can make the difference between a smooth job and a frustrating one.

Marking tools

Good

Pencils make layout marks on the wall that won't show through in the final paint or wallpapering job—and can be erased if you mismark.

Bad

Felt-tip markers and ink pens make marks that will bleed through paints and wallpapers.

Alignment tools

Good

Plumb lines and laser lines give you perfectly vertical lines.

Bad

Levels are less accurate than plumb lines and laser lines and are harder to use.

Openers

Good

A 10-in-1 tool (another version is the 5-in-1 tool) is designed to open a can of paint without damaging the can lid. This is one of my favorite tools.

Bad

Can keys and screwdrivers often damage the lip of the can, allowing air to get in and ruin the contents.

Knives

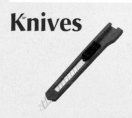

Good

Snap-blade knives are slender, lightweight, and brightly colored and allow you to use a fresh blade for every cut on wallpaper or masking tape.

Bad

Utility knives are larger, more cumbersome, and easier to lose and require more time to change blades.

Sanding tools

Good

Synthetic scouring pads are easy to rinse clean, are long-lasting, and can be used wet for practically dustless smoothing of spackle and drywall compound when repairing walls.

Bad

Traditional sanding blocks create dust, and the abrasive clogs easily and must be replaced often, adding expense and time to the job.

Seam setting tools

Good

A plastic float or seam smoother is comfortable in your hand, puts even pressure on the seam, and will not squeeze the adhesive out of the seam.

Bad

A seam roller applies too much pressure to the seam, leaving indentations in the wallpapered surface. It also squeezes out the adhesive, resulting in lifting seams.

Broad knives

Good

A 4-inch broad knife makes an excellent guide when trimming wallpaper after application and is small enough to fit in a work pouch.

Bad

An 8-inch broad knife is unwieldy to work with comfortably, blocks your vision as you're trimming, and reduces accuracy when cutting around irregular profiles such as moldings.

Ladders

Good

An aluminum platform ladder is lightweight and comfortable to stand on, allows you to get close to the wall, and offers a shelf to hold tools.

Bad

A 5-foot stepladder is heavy and uncomfortable to stand on and places you too far from the wall to work efficiently.

Smoothing tools

Good

A wallpaper brush applies even pressure to the wallpaper while you are applying sheets to the wall and fits easily in your hand and tool pouch.

Bad

A sponge can drag the wallpaper out of alignment and mar the wallpaper surface.

Some painting tips are summarized here for easy reference.

Painting like a pro

Slide a metal roller tray into a heavy-duty tall plastic kitchen bag, then press the bag into the tray to create a liner. If you need to stop, fold the liner over the tray to keep the paint from drying. The bag liner makes cleanup a cinch; simply turn the bag inside out and toss it in the trash.

Take the "pain" out of painting. To avoid carpal tunnel syndrome, blisters, and cramps, make a soft grip for your paintbrush. Take 2-inch diameter pipe insulation, trim to the right length, and shove it over the handle of your paintbrush.

If you need to temporarily stop painting, protect the paint in your bucket or roller tray by slipping a plastic shower cap or plastic bowl cover over it. The cover keeps debris and air out. Put brushes in a resealable plastic bag. Tie closed the plastic trash bag you've used to line your paint bucket.

Line your paint pot with a large resealable plastic bag. Open the mouth of the bag and fold down over the edge of the bucket rim. Secure with a large rubber band. If you need to pause from painting, zip the bag closed to prevent drying.

Paint the trim work first, then the walls. This strategy will make it easier to sand, prepare, and paint all the details, edges, and planes of the trim work. After all the coats of paint on the trim work are dry, mask off the trim work and paint the wall.

Build some bucket stilts.
See page 35.

For the best finish on trim, apply two thin coats of paint rather than one heavy coat. The first thin coat dries faster and bonds better to the surface. The second coat deepens the color coverage. With one heavy coat you run the risk of the paint sagging, creating a poor finish quality.

To keep latex paint off your body, apply nonstick cooking spray onto your skin and rub it in. Water-based paint can't penetrate the oil, so the paint won't seep through your skin. I figure, if you can eat it, you can wear it. Just make sure you use the original flavor spray—not the garlic version!

Don't like the smell of paint? To every quart of interior latex paint, add four drops of vanilla extract.

You can also use other extracts, such as peppermint, as long as the alcohol in the ingredients is methyl alcohol, which is formulated to mix with water. Do not use perfume or other alcohol-based fragrances.

Paint over textured surfaces with a foam roller. This type of roller will unload a lot of paint on an irregular surface. The foam conforms to the surface it is rolling on, working paint into all the nooks and crannies, producing even surface coverage.

Make a handy painting tool belt. See page 34.

Remove masking materials within 45 to 90 minutes after the paint is applied and set to prevent tearing the surface. When paint flows over the sealed edge of masking tape, then hardens, the paint film bonds to both the wall and the tape. It's easier to remask an area than to repair it!

Make a paint tray trolley. Buy a large square plant dolly with casters, four 4- to 6-inch plastic spring clamps, and a length of 2-inch foam pipe insulation. Center an empty paint tray to the plant mover and use a pencil to outline where the tray will be used. At the four points of the outline, secure a spring clamp to the plant dolly with screws. Make a wall bumper by applying the pipe insulation around the edge of the plant mover. To use, place a paint tray on the dolly and clamp it in place.

chapter 3

Preparation

The natural inclination with any project is to jump right in and start the work so you can see some results—preferably within a few hours. But take it from the Wall Wizard: The success of any home improvement project depends on preparation. And that's especially true for painting, faux finishing, and installing wallpaper.

About 80 percent of the work done by any professional decorating contractor is preparation. All room surfaces must be cleaned, repaired, and smoothed. You will put in one to three hours of prep time for every hour you spend actually applying paint or wallpaper.

I know it sounds like drudgery and lots of work. And you know what—it is! But believe me, the time spent properly prepping a room will more than repay itself in a quicker, smoother, more professional job. Here's why:

- A clean, cleared-out room is safer and easier to work in than one cluttered with furnishings—and your work will go much faster too.

- Proper preparation avoids damaging floors, walls, woodwork, and built-ins both before and during the application process—and makes cleanup afterward easy.

- Clean surfaces in good condition are the foundation for good adhesion, so wallpaper is less likely to peel, curl, bubble, or discolor.

- Smooth surfaces ensure that when you're done, you'll see the paint or wallpaper—not the imperfections underneath.

Ready the ROOM

You've probably tried to work around furniture and carpeting during decorating projects, but it always happens: You dribble or spill on something. That's why step one in prep work is to clear out the room.

● An empty room is an easy room to work in, so begin by removing everything that you can. Gather anything that is left to one side of the room, away from your work area.

● Next, turn off the power to any outlets or fixtures on the surfaces you will be working on.

● Then remove all light fixtures, switch and outlet plates, heat registers, and towel rods—anything you will have to paint or apply wallpaper around. This includes drapes (get them cleaned while they are down) and drapery hardware. Don't try to work around the hardware; it is too frustrating and time-consuming. Just pay particular attention to how your window treatments are attached and make a diagram, if necessary, so you can reinstall them correctly and without guesswork.

● Loosen the canopy or trim piece of a ceiling fixture or chandelier and slide it down the fixture away from the ceiling. Wrap it with plastic trash bags or plastic wrap. Never unscrew a fixture from the electrical box and allow it to hang by its wires. The wires aren't meant to hold a fixture's weight; there's the immediate danger of falling glass fixtures, as well as the risk that the wires could be damaged, creating an electrical short and a fire hazard later. A ceiling fan is impossible to paint around, so take it down.

● After removing switch and outlet plates, be sure to protect the switches and outlets themselves with blue masking tape to shield them from solvents, cleaners, paint, wallpaper adhesive, and moisture.

● Place a worktable in another room, or outside if you will be using solvents. You can make a table by laying a piece of plywood or a flush wooden door over two sawhorses.

● Starting thinking now: Cleanup is not what you do at the end of the job, it's what you do throughout your project. Place a large, lined trash can in the room to throw away debris as you work. A messy workplace is unsafe and can slow you down.

tips 'n' tricks

I used to have a bad habit of laying switch plates on the floor and losing them under the drop cloth, until I'd step down and hear "crunch!" Then my wife came up with a brilliant use for resealable storage bags. As you disassemble the room, drop all the switch plates into one medium plastic bag. Remount screws back into their fixtures so they don't get lost or scratch the plastic plates. Separate the hardware for each window, door, and curtain into its own bag and mark its location in the room. Once all the hardware has been bagged and tagged, place the bags into one large bag with the room name on it. For safekeeping, stick the bag on the windowpane of the room with blue tape.

At every home show someone asks me how to remove wallpaper. It's the no. 1 technique people want to learn. It's a simple job—reverse hanging, actually. Ideally the paper should pull off the wall in fully intact sheets rather than the 4-inch strips created by a wallpaper scraper. Sound like magic? A bit of wizardry will help you remove wallpaper with ease.

The trick to removing an old wallpaper is to use tools and techniques that won't damage the surface or shred the wallpaper while dissolving the adhesive that bonds the wallpaper to the wall. Wallpaper adhesives are based on simple starch binders. For easy removal, mix a special solution (see page 49) that will attack the starch bonds between the wall and the paper.

The Solution

In my Secret Stripping Solution (see page 49), water carries enzymes (the remover) that eat starch. Liquid fabric softener is a surfactant that makes the water wetter. When you add vinegar (a mild acid) and baking soda (a base) together, they create a carbonic gas reaction that turbocharges the solution. Placing a plastic sheet over the wall forces saturated solution through the holes made by the Paper Tiger. The solution is trapped under a sealed, nonporous plastic sheet that prevents it from drying, so the water-based solution can slowly break down the starch bonds that hold the wallpaper to the surface. TSP is an alkaline salt with a low pH value that needs to be neutralized by a mild acid-rinsing agent, such as white vinegar.

wizard WARNING

Thinking about installing new wallpaper right over the old? Think again! Sure, you avoid the mess of removing the wallpaper, but the resulting finish is not as good. The old wallpaper's patterns and seam lines often show through the new material. Applying wallpaper paste to old paper can soften it and weaken its bond to the wall, potentially causing your new wallpaper to peel off. And it can be tough to clean dirt, grease, and other nasty stuff from old, porous wallpaper, which can prevent the new wallpaper from bonding well.

Dry removal

Fabric-backed vinyl or strippable solid-surface vinyl can often be removed using a dry stripping method.

1. Begin by peeling the top edge of a sheet of vinyl wallpaper away from the wall about 2 inches. Hold a dowel or broom handle against the wall and roll the paper around it in spool fashion.

2. Continue rolling the dowel down the wall, removing and rolling the paper as you work. The dowel keeps the pressure spread evenly across the sheet of paper, which can help prevent tearing. When you reach the bottom of the wall, slide the vinyl off the dowel and discard it. Start removing the next strip with a bare dowel. There are two types of vinyl wallpaper: solid vinyl or vinyl with a paper backing. If you're working with the latter, the vinyl will come off on your dowel roller, leaving the paper behind. Strip the paper backing with the wet-strip method after the vinyl is removed.

Secret Stripping Solution

3 gallons hot water
22 ounces wallpaper remover concentrate with enzymes
¼ cup liquid fabric softener
1 cup white vinegar
2 tablespoons baking soda

Wet removal

Use this method to remove more than one layer of wallpaper at a time. (I've removed more than a dozen layers at once this way.)

1. Turn off power to the room and remove the electrical cover plates. Place a strip of waterproof duct tape over the exposed electrical plugs and switches to shield them from water. You're going to be using a lot of water in this process, so cover the floors with plastic sheeting and an absorbent drop cloth or old towels. Secure the plastic sheeting along the edge of moldings with duct tape. The goal is to create a waterproof catch basin to avoid damaging the flooring. Change the absorbent drop cloth or towels frequently to ensure your floor stays dry.

2. Perforate the wallpaper with a Paper Tiger (to save time, you can use two Paper Tigers—one in each hand). The rotary teeth penetrate the surface of the wallpaper, allowing the solution to soak through and soften the adhesive. Start at the top left corner of the wall and work down and across the wall, making large circles. Poke about 10 holes per square inch—enough to perforate, but not shred, the paper.

3. Pour the stripping solution into a clean garden sprayer, pressurize it, and adjust the nozzle for a medium mist. Spray the walls from the bottom up, working around the room in one direction. Apply the solution at least three times around the room. Mix a fresh batch as needed. To ensure that the chemical reaction is working effectively, move quickly; the solution remains active for only about 15 minutes.

4. When the walls are thoroughly saturated, smooth 0.7-mil plastic sheeting over the entire surface with a wallpaper brush and cut the plastic around the moldings to create a vacuum-tight seal. The secret is to trap the solution under the plastic. Leave the plastic on at least three hours—overnight is better—allowing the solution to dissolve the adhesive.

5. To test whether the adhesive has released, pull back a lower corner of the plastic and gently scrape the wallpaper from a corner with a paper scraper to see if it is loose enough for removal. If the wallpaper resists, carefully lift the plastic about 6 inches away at the top of the wall in small areas and spray more solution to resoak the wallpaper. Then smooth the plastic back and let the solution work for an additional 6 to 12 hours. Allow the process to dissolve the adhesive by keeping it wet, and you'll be rewarded by wallpaper that's very easy to remove.

6. When the adhesive has softened enough to remove the paper, fold about 4 feet of the plastic back toward a corner of the wall. Stick pushpins in the folded plastic so it doesn't fall down. Strip only one section at a time. Starting at the top of the wallpapering, lift the edge and begin scraping the wet paper backing off the wall. Position the scraping tool at a low attack angle to reduce surface gouging and damage. Spray on more stripping solution to keep the paper moist; work from the top down, left to right. When that section is completely removed, fold back the next section of plastic and remove the wallpaper as described in the previous steps. Discard the stripped wallpaper into a garbage can lined with a plastic trash bag to keep the slippery, gooey mess off the floor.

Other removal methods

Gel remover clings to the paper. It is especially effective for removing borders. Perforate the surface in the same manner as for wet removal, then apply the gel. Give it time to work properly in dissolving the wallpapering adhesive. Clean and rinse.

Steam removal is more dangerous than other methods, and it can damage the drywall behind the paper. If you do use a steam remover, perforate the surface in the same manner as for wet removal, then follow the manufacturer's instructions.

tips 'n' tricks

Old adhesive left on the wall can prevent new wallpapering from sticking successfully. The iodine test shows if you have removed all adhesive. Mix 1 ounce of iodine with 1 quart of water and pour into a trigger-spray bottle. Spray the area where the wallpapering has been removed. If the iodine turns bluish purple, continue cleaning. Test again until you don't see any color on the wall. Spray the solution sparingly, as iodine can stain if overused.

My Mistake
WHAT GOES UP CAN COME DOWN—FAST!

Whenever I get a new platform ladder, I always apply self-stick traction strips to the steps so I don't slip and fall. Aluminum is slippery enough—add a layer of water on top of it, and it can be like ice.

Well, I learned the hard way that you need to remove the old traction strips and apply new ones when the strips' adhesive starts to fail or the rough surface starts to wear. I was climbing my trusty platform ladder for the half-millionth time since I'd bought it, carrying a strip of wallpapering in both hands. Naturally, some of the water and wallpapering adhesive dripped onto the ladder step—right in the middle of where the traction strip had worn nearly through. I slipped, my feet went out from under me in a flash, and even though I was just on the first rung, barely a foot off the floor, my chin hit the top of the ladder on the way down and I knocked myself out. The liquid that caused me to slip and fall could just as easily have been paint or glaze.

I woke up 10 minutes later with a huge gash on my chin and blood all over the floor. Fortunately, I was on linoleum so I didn't ruin somebody's carpet. But the scar remains to remind me to this day.

Lesson learned: Check your safety equipment periodically to make sure it still works. This goes not only for worn traction strips or cane tips on ladders, but worn, cracked, or slit insulation on extension cords, heat guards on work lights, lenses on goggles (if they're dirty, you're less likely to wear them), and cartridges on respirators.

CLEANING the Walls

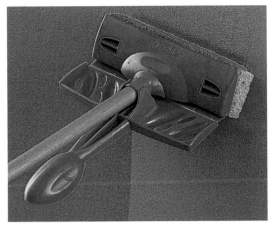

Washing

Scrubbing

Cleaning a surface before applying a new finish is just as important as any other step. That's because paint and wallpaper are films: Anything on the wall that's biologically or chemically active will come through eventually and ruin your job.

Mildew, oil, and grease prevent paint and wallpaper adhesives from bonding. Rust and water stains will show through. Even the most expensive finishes are only as good as the surface to which you apply them.

An empty room is an easy room to work in. When everything has been removed, clean the floor and baseboards. Cover the floor with plastic sheeting, securing the edges to the floor with duct tape. Then add a layer of drop cloths. Cover any remaining furnishings with 0.7-mil plastic sheeting.

After washing a wall, allow it to dry for a day before you apply wallpaper. This job is much easier when one person scrubs and another rinses.

First, dust off all surfaces with a vacuum cleaner or sweep with a clean dust mop. Ventilate the room well. Wash the walls with a sponge-head mop and denatured alcohol; work in 8-foot widths, from the bottom up, working around the room. When you reach your starting point, turn the mop head around and begin scrubbing the wall with the nylon scrubbing head.

After scrubbing the first 8-foot section, wipe the wall with a cloth saturated in denatured alcohol to remove dirt.

wizard WARNING

Completely remove any old wallpaper adhesive before you apply new wallpaper or paint. If you can't remove all the adhesive, apply an oil sealer over the entire wall surface. Do not use a latex primer—latex, like wallpaper adhesive, is water-based. The latex paint will reanimate the old adhesive, creating a crackle finish to which new wallpaper adhesive will not bond. Two thin coats of oil sealer, on the other hand, provide a uniform, waterproof bond that will prevent the new adhesive from reanimating the old adhesive. When you apply the sealer, brush or roll it onto the area first horizontally, then vertically for full coverage. Spot priming isn't good enough—the moisture from the new adhesive can migrate around the primed spot, causing the primer to fail from underneath.

Mold and mildew

Regardless of where you live, you may be plagued with mold and mildew. Look for splotches on your walls. If you find some, dab them with a small amount of household bleach. If the spot comes off, it's not dirt—it is mold or mildew.

1. To remove mold and mildew, mix 1 cup household cleaner and 2 cups hydrogen peroxide in 1 gallon warm water. Wear gloves and goggles. Apply the solution with a sponge or mop and let stand for several minutes. Several applications may be needed. Rinse with a solution of 1 cup vinegar in a gallon of water.

2. When dry, lightly sand the places where the mildew appeared.

3. Seal against another outbreak by applying two coats of white-pigmented oil-based sealer. Sand lightly between coats.

Grease stains

Stubborn grease stains require an additional cleaning step. To remove, rub them with a liquid deglosser to break the oil film. When dry, sand with 120-grit paper, then wipe away the sanding dust. Seal with two coats of white-pigmented oil-based sealer. Sand lightly between coats.

Rust and water stains

Rust and water stains will show through paint. To remove these spots, scrub with a solution of ¼ cup Epsom salts in 1 cup warm water. Rinse with a mixture of 1 cup vinegar in a gallon of warm water. Allow to dry for several days, then sand with 120-grit sandpaper. Seal with two coats of white-pigmented oil-based sealer. Sand lightly between coats.

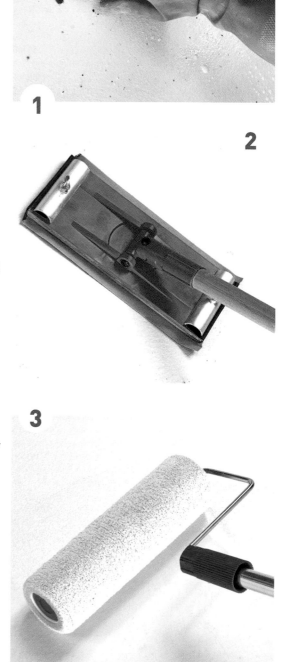

1

2

3

tips 'n' tricks

Think your walls are grime-free? Try this test: Spray a tissue with water and lightly rub it on the wall. See that brown smudge? It's body oils, hair spray, and food oils that become airborne while cooking and eventually settle on the walls. Many wallpapering and painting jobs fail because wallpaper and paint are applied on top of dingy, dirty surfaces. Clean before you cover.

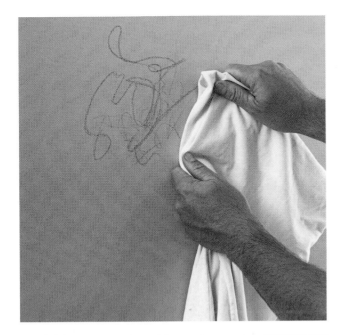

Marker and crayon stains

With three children, I've tackled more than my share of crayon marks on the wall. The best way to remove these stains is to fold an old T-shirt into a pad several layers thick and place it over a crayon mark, then run an iron set at medium heat over the pad (top and center). If it doesn't remove the mark entirely, heat the mark with a hair dryer and blot away as much of the mark as possible (bottom). Seal with two coats of white-pigmented oil-based sealer, sanding lightly between coats.

For scribbles from permanent markers, lightly dab the spot with nail polish remover. Rub the spot with a liquid deglosser. When dry, sand with 120-grit paper, then wipe away the sanding dust. Seal with two coats of white-pigmented oil-based sealer. Sand between coats.

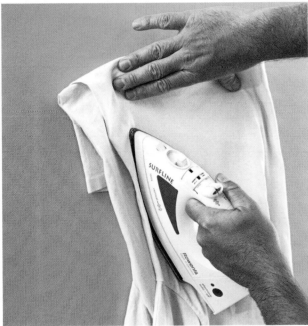

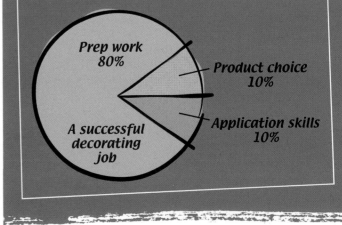

quiz the WIZ

Can't I just wipe the wall down and start applying?

I cannot stress enough how important it is to prep your walls before applying paint or wallpaper. Sure, you can start applying without taking the time to follow through on prep work, but you're going to waste time and money because the material won't bond to or hide any of the imperfections on the wall. If you don't prep your walls, good luck—you're going to need it!

Prep work 80%

Product choice 10%

Application skills 10%

A successful decorating job

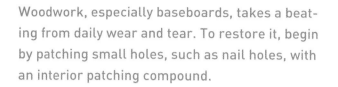

WOOD Work

Woodwork, especially baseboards, takes a beating from daily wear and tear. To restore it, begin by patching small holes, such as nail holes, with an interior patching compound.

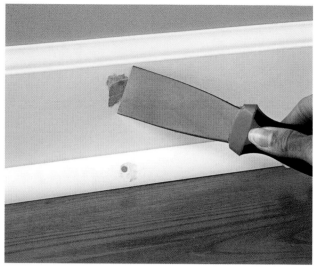

Sand the patched areas smooth using 180-grit paper, then lightly sand the entire surface. Vacuum the woodwork, then wipe it with a tack cloth to remove dust. Seal the entire surface and paint it.

If the woodwork has sustained extensive damage and the moldings have stock profiles (standard profiles typically stocked by lumber yards and home improvement stores), it is probably easier and faster simply to remove the damaged woodwork and replace it with new molding. Use a small prybar to loosen the molding; place a scrap piece of wood behind the prybar for better leverage and to prevent damage to pieces you might want to save. Use pliers to remove nails; it's usually easier to pull them through the pieces, rather than trying to hammer them back out.

If the woodwork is clear-finished rather than painted, fill holes and defects with a matching wood filler or stainable latex wood putty. Before staining, apply a sanding sealer. The sealer helps better match the stain that you are applying to the existing stain. Then stain the patched areas for trim that will receive a clear finish. After staining, apply two thin coats of clear finish.

If the moldings in your house are antique or custom-milled, you'll need to have them professionally restored or have new moldings custom-milled. In that case, consult a professional finish carpenter.

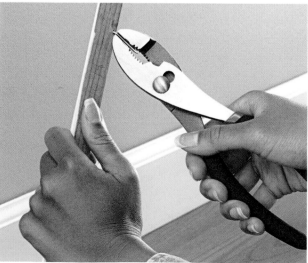

REPAIRING Drywall Imperfections

I've seen this happen in both old and new houses: As the drywall settles it develops noticeable cracks, especially at stress points. Age can also open joints and expose popped nails. Don't let these routine repairs stress you out. I've developed easy methods to fix drywall problems once and for all.

Repairing popped nails

1. Drive a 1¼-inch wallboard screw into the stud or joist about 2 inches from the popped nail so the head is slightly recessed. The screw should pull the wallboard tight against the framing.

2. Drive the popped nail down into the drywall.

3. With a 6-inch broad knife, cover the nail hole and screw head with lightweight surfacing compound. Let dry overnight; lightly wet-sand. Apply a thin second coat. Let it dry overnight.

4. Apply two coats of white-pigmented sealer to seal the porous surfacing compound. This also keeps the paint sheen consistent, promotes proper adhesion for paint or wallpaper, and keeps color variations from showing through.

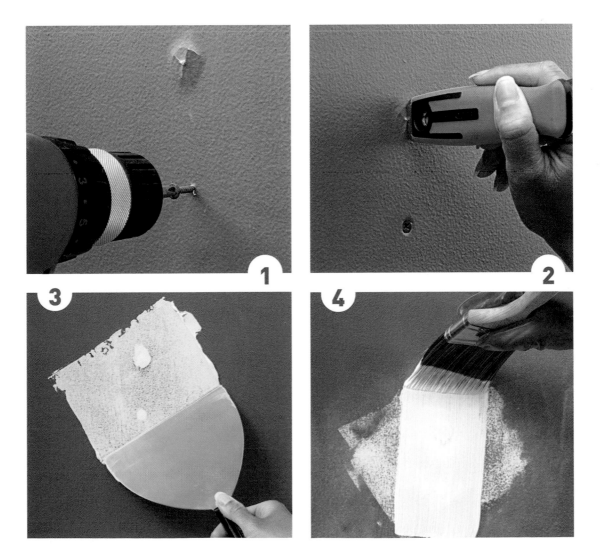

Crack attack

Stress-point cracks are hard to repair permanently because they can reappear when the house shifts. The secret to filling such cracks is to use an interior vinyl spackling paste, which remains flexible, so it expands and contracts with the house.

1. If the crack is more than a hairline fissure but narrower than ¼ inch, widen it slightly and undercut its sides with a 10-in-1 tool. Vacuum, sponge, or brush out the crack to remove all the gypsum powder and paper.

2. With a 6-inch broad knife, apply interior vinyl surfacing compound using an overlapping technique and let dry. Sand with 120-grit sandpaper or wet-sand.

3. Reinforce the patched joint along its entire length with self-adhesive fiberglass-mesh or moistened paper joint tape. Apply more of the surfacing compound over the tape and let dry. If necessary, sand again and apply a third coat with a wider knife.

4. Sand the patch and allow to dry.

5. Seal the repair with two coats of white-pigmented sealer.

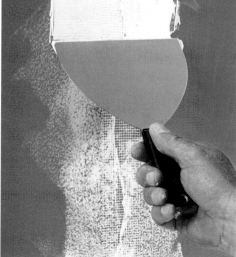

PATCHING Small Holes

The devil's in the details—your eye is drawn to imperfections, so it's worth correcting even the slightest flaws in your walls before you start decorating.

1. Spackle small holes in drywall or plaster by pressing the filler into the hole with a putty knife. Don't overfill. Two thin coats are better than one thick one.

2. To patch holes 1 to 4 inches across, such as a doorknob ding, put fiberglass-mesh reinforcing tape over the hole, then apply two coats of surfacing compound over the patch, letting it dry between coats. Sand lightly between coats.

3. To make quick work of sealing small repairs, use an aerosol can of quick-drying sealer, applied with a trigger sprayer. The spray can means quick coverage with no cleanup; the trigger makes it easy to apply.

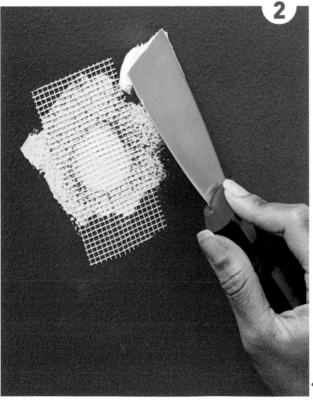

wizard WARNING

Hear the one about using toothpaste to fill holes in the wall? Don't do it! Toothpaste doesn't dry hard, can't be sanded, won't hold up over time, is water-soluble, and may contain bleaches that will stain any paint or wallpaper applied over it.

Repairing Large HOLES

Need to repair a large hole, such as the one made when a doorknob gets pushed right through a wall? You deserve a wave of the Wizard's wand just for tackling the project! Large holes require a bit more patience and care to fix. Follow these directions, though, and you'll do fine.

1. Measure the hole. Cut a piece of drywall large enough to cover it. Trace around the patch onto the wall and, with a drywall saw, cut out the marked area. If the patch is large enough to extend from one stud to another, cut the opening to the center of each stud so you'll have nailing surfaces for the patch.

2. Cut one or more backer strips out of 1×2 boards, plywood, or drywall scraps. Make them 3 to 4 inches longer than the hole.

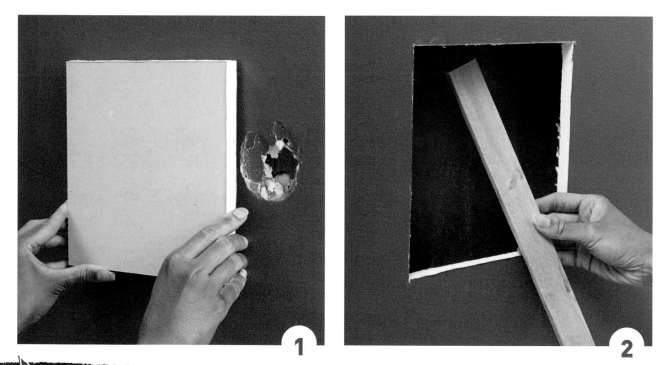

sanding

Sanding is the key to a flawless painting or wallpapering job, especially if you've done any wall patching or other repairs. In most situations light dry-sanding will be enough to remove peaks of patching material and polish the surface. A wallboard sanding screen, handheld sanding block, or power sander works well for large jobs. Don't use a belt sander; it will abrade the surface too much.

Sand drywall and plaster along the longest direction. Wear a respirator and seal off the room to keep dust from spreading. Place a box fan in the window so it will suck fine dust out of the room and exhaust it outside. This works best if you open another window or door—ideally on a wall opposite the fan—to ensure cross-ventilation and a good supply of clean air.

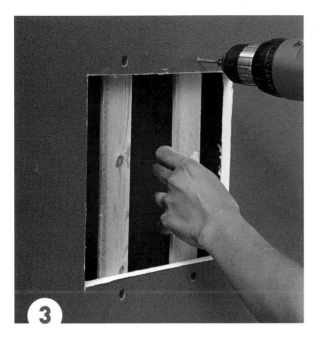

3. Slip the backer strips behind the opening and secure them to the wall with 1-inch wallboard screws. Lightly coat the edges of the hole and the patch with joint compound. Push the patch into the opening and fasten it to the backer strips with drywall screws. If the ends lay on studs, fasten the patch to the studs as well.

4. Apply strips of self-adhesive fiberglass-mesh tape or moistened paper joint tape to the seams, overlapping the tape at the corners of the patch. Work a coat of joint compound into and over the tape, making horizontal and vertical sweeps. This is called the *crisscross technique.* Let dry overnight. Sand with 120-grit sandpaper. Skim a second coat of compound over the entire patch. Let the patch dry completely.

5. Sand with 120-grit sandpaper and seal with white-pigmented oil-based sealer.

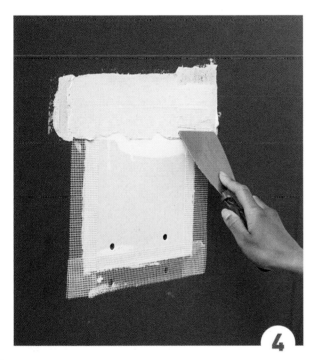

patching on white

When patching white walls or molding, mix two drops of red food coloring into every 6 ounces of surfacing compound to make it easy to spot repairs for sanding later.

My Mistake

TWO PEOPLE CAN BE STUPID AT THE SAME TIME, SO TRIPLE YOUR SAFETY PRECAUTIONS.

I used to turn off all the light switches in a room before working there, then turn off the power at the breaker box. "That way," I thought, "I'm doubly protected." True enough, but sometimes double just isn't enough.

Once, after my apprentice and I had finished applying wallpaper in a master suite, I was reinstalling the lights in a bathroom while my apprentice was reattaching the outlet and switch plates in the adjoining bedroom. He finished first and went to the breaker box to turn the bedroom power back on. He inadvertently restored the current to the bathroom as well.

Not good, but not horrible either. He'd defeated only one of my safety precautions, and so far, no current to the wires.

Then, just as I was attaching the last two wires together with a wire nut, he walked into the bathroom and flipped the switch on.

"Yee-ow!" wasn't all I had to say about it.

Lesson learned: Use as many safety precautions as you can. Now I turn off the switch, turn off the circuit breaker, and tape the switch in the "off" position.

Mudding TEXTURED Walls

2

3

4

Sometimes it's impractical to install drywall over a textured surface: The room may be small and awkward to work in, for instance. Or delicate moldings, trimwork, or other built-in features may not allow you to add a sheet material to the surface without dramatically changing the character of the room.

Rather than sanding the texture from a wall, it is easier to fill in, or float, over the texture that exists. This technique is known as *mudding*.

1. Clear out the room and clean the walls.

2. Lightly sand the entire wall with a pole sander and a 120-grit sanding screen to knock down any roughness or high peaks on the wall. This drastically reduces the time and material you'll need to achieve a smooth surface. Do not scrape textured surfaces. Dust the walls with a clean broom or vacuum.

   If there are any damaged areas on the wall, spot-seal the areas by applying two coats of white-pigmented oil-based sealer to the wall. Use a disposable brush or a roller with a disposable cover. Let dry, which will take 45 minutes to 1 hour. Sand lightly with a 120-grit sanding screen.

3. Thin premix joint compound with water in a 5-gallon bucket until it is the consistency of a heavy meringue. Adding water makes the compound more liquid to improve the flow. Mix thoroughly to a uniform consistency using a drill equipped with a propeller-type drywall compound mixing tool. Don't use a mixer designed for paint—it won't adequately stir the compound, which is thicker than paint.

4. Before applying compound, divide the wall into 4-foot-square sections. Scoop the compound into a stainless-steel or plastic drywall tray.

5. Sharpen the edge of your drywall knife by moving it back and forth briskly across the surface of your drywall sander. This removes any rust from the broad knife so it doesn't stain the mud, which can show through to the final finish. This polishing also removes any dings or imperfections in the edge of the blade.

6. Wash and rinse dirt and metal shavings off the blade using a clean tile sponge dipped in a bucket of clean water. Do this after you've completed each 4×4 section of wall to prevent dried mud from building up on the blade and to keep the blade wet so the mud flows smoothly from blade to wall. When working with mud, wetter is better.

7. Apply mud to the wall with 4-foot-long horizontal strokes. This is called *laying on.* Strive for a relatively even coat but don't worry about creating a perfectly smooth finish at this stage.

8. Scrape off excess mud that may remain on your broad knife. Then stroke the mud vertically from top to bottom, working from left to right to create a crosshatch effect. This makes a thin, even coat without the ridges that can result from stroking in only one direction. As you're making the final stroke, angle the broad knife slightly in the direction you're moving it to avoid leaving ridges in the mud.

tips 'n' tricks

Wetter is better! The cleaner you keep your tools, the better your job will be. And in this case, clean means wet. If you keep your tools wet, mud won't dry on the tool, build up, and roughen the edge, which creates streaks in your finish. Working wet also prevents dried chunks of mud from flaking off the tool and embedding themselves in the finish, creating more streaks or divots as you move the tool over them. Those streaks or divots will require an additional coat of mud to correct, prolonging the job.

9. Feather the mud into corners by running the broad knife vertically down the wall with a nice, even stroke. Bring the broad knife as close to the adjacent wall surface as possible without actually touching it. This helps avoid ripples and ridges in the finish caused by texture on the adjacent wall.

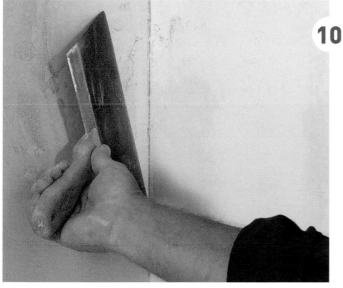

10. Let the wall dry overnight, then scrape off any ridges by moving a sharp broad knife back and forth over the surface at a low angle. This process is called *kerfing*.

11. Wet-sand the surface using a green scouring pad and a bucket of clean water. Dip the pad in the water, then wring it until it is damp but not dripping. Move it in a gentle circular motion over the surface to knock down the high spots. This also fills low spots with a paste made of excess material removed from the high spots mixed with the moisture in the sponge. A sponge that's too wet will simply wash the material off the wall. Leave as much material on the wall as possible while smoothing the surface for the next application.

quiz the WIZ

Why should I put on several thin coats of mud when I could put on a one thick coat and sand the excess off?

There are lots of reasons: Thick coats can sag, creating bulges and wrinkles. They take forever to dry. But the main reason not to apply one thick coat is that doing so requires power sanding, which creates a fine, abrasive dust that permeates everything, making a mess of your house.

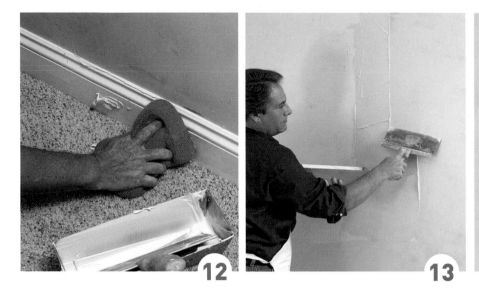

12. Clean as you go. Drywall mud is much easier to clean up when it's wet—you can just wipe up an errant dollop with a sponge. After it dries you have to chisel or sand it off.

13. Two thin coats are better than one thick one. After your wet-sanding job on the first coat has dried, apply a second coat. Note how the angle at which I'm holding the broad knife results in a ridge of excess material on one side of the knife only.

14. Let the second coat dry and wet-sand it as you did with the first coat. This time, use a slightly finer-grit white scouring pad. Lightly polish the surface; don't abrade it severely.

15. Use a dish scrubber filled with water to work into corners and around moldings. The hollow handle gives you reach and leverage and allows you to slightly dampen the scrubbing surface with water whenever it gets a bit too dry.

tips 'n' tricks

The bane of every home remodeling job is drywall dust. It's insidious stuff—very fine and very messy. It gets into everything—your carpets, your fabrics, your ductwork and furnace filters, everything. So one of the main goals in mudding is to create a smooth finish that minimizes the need for sanding afterwards. Whenever you can, wet-sand rather than dry-sand. Wet-sanding goes a long way toward minimizing dust. And it creates a smoother finish with less work because the process actually adds drywall compound to low spots while removing it from high spots. And that means you typically can apply fewer coats of mud to get the same effect compared with dry-sanding, which only removes high spots.

REMOVING Ceiling Texture

Now that you've smoothed the walls, why stop there? If your house was built in recent decades, chances are you have a textured "popcorn" ceiling. I hate the stuff! It traps dust, turning your ceiling gray or black around heating and air-conditioning vents, it's difficult to paint, and pieces crumble and fall off if you brush against it. That can result in crumbs of texture falling between your wallpaper and the wall as you install wallpaper, creating irregularities in the surface. I say get rid of it now, while the room is cleared out and your tools are at hand.

Remove any nonasbestos texturing by soaking it with a solution of 1 cup ammonia and 1 cup fabric softener added to 1 gallon water. This procedure can make a big mess, so cover the floor well with taped-down plastic before you start. Apply the solution with a spray bottle or garden sprayer and let it soak in for about 15 minutes. Then scrape the softened texture off the ceiling with a floor squeegee.

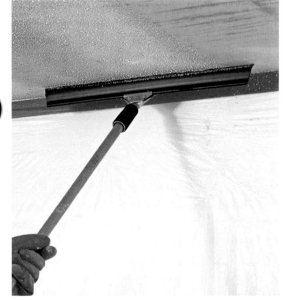

wizard WARNING

A textured ceiling, especially one that was sprayed before 1970, could contain asbestos. For that reason alone, do not attempt to remove the texture if you are not sure whether asbestos is present. Always assume texture material contains asbestos until a test proves otherwise. For more information, see page 73.

cool tool

A clever way to dispose of old popcorn ceilings is to scrape the texture material directly into a homemade catch-bag. Cut a 20-inch-diameter circle in the center of a 24-inch-diameter plastic trash can lid. On the remaining plastic rim, cut an X into the plastic. Insert the long handle of a squeegee into the X and attach a 10-gallon plastic trash bag over the center hole; secure with standard spring clips. Now when you pull the squeegee across the ceiling, the popcorn will drop into the bag, eliminating much of the mess.

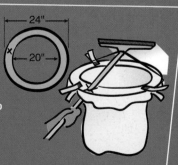

You can cover a ceiling with drywall the same way you would a wall.

If you are installing more than a half-dozen ceiling panels, consider renting a wallboard jack. This device raises or lowers a full sheet of drywall with a simple crank. It has wheels so you can position the wallboard easily. With a jack, one person can install ceiling panels.

To hang just a few wallboard sheets, use a T-support. You can make one yourself for a couple of bucks and it will save you two trips to the rental store. Cut one 2×4 about 40 inches long. Cut another piece to a length equal to the distance from the floor to the ceiling of the room, minus 1 inch plus the thickness of the wallboard (1½ inches for ½-inch drywall). Fasten the long piece to the center of the short one at a right angle. Add braces for strength. Hold the support so the cross member of the T is near the ceiling, with the T's leg resting on the floor at an angle. With helpers, position a sheet of drywall on the ceiling, then move the leg of the brace toward the vertical until the T's cross member holds the wallboard snug against the ceiling.

Before installation, use a stud finder to locate the ceiling joists. Mark the location of each joist on the top of an adjacent wall with a light pencil mark so you'll know where to place fasteners when installing the ceiling panels. Install panels parallel to joists. If possible, use panels long enough to span from wall to wall.

Lift the first panel into place and attach it through the existing ceiling surface and into the joists with 1¾-inch type W wallboard screws using a drill/driver. Begin in

the center of the panel and work outward. Stagger any unavoidable end joints at least 16 inches. If you cut any panels full length, place the cut edge against the wall and leave a slight gap. Place screws no closer than ⅜ inch to panel edges. Set screw heads just below the surface of the panel, but do not break through the paper facing. If a screw head does break through the paper, place another screw right next to it. Embed screwheads far enough into the paper for joint compound to cover them. Tape and finish the drywall joints.

The Great COVER-UP

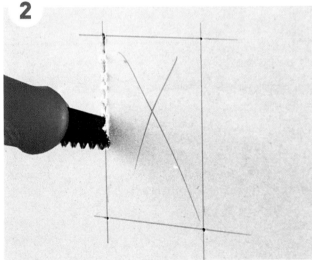

Cut holes for electrical boxes using a drywall saw. Its point can poke through drywall to start the cut, but you can drill holes at the corners of the cutout to make it a little easier. You may need to use box extenders to bring the edge of the switch box flush with the new wall surface.

The best, and in many ways easiest, coverup for textured walls or paneling is to install new ¼- or ⅜-inch drywall over them.

Drywall sheets are 4 feet wide and commonly available in lengths of 8 or 10 feet (⅜ inch can also be found in 12- or 14-foot lengths). Measure your wall and determine the size of the sheets and their arrangement on the wall (horizontal or vertical) to create the fewest seams and the fewest partial sheets possible. Don't place new seams directly over old seams.

Moisture-resistant drywall panels are good for use in kitchens or bathrooms. Use drywall screws or ring-shank nails to secure the sheets in place. If you are attaching directly to old gypsum wallboard, use Type G screws. You can also use construction adhesive and fasteners to hold up the new panels.

1. Remove all the woodwork from the surface, both at the top and the bottom of the walls. Mark the location of all the wall studs so you can easily find them as you install the new drywall sheets. Place a light pencil mark on the ceiling at the point of each stud. Mark the locations of electrical boxes.

2. Use a utility knife to cut through the outside face of drywall and into the gypsum. Guide the cut with a drywall T-square or a carpenter's square. Make two or three passes to deepen the cut; you don't have to cut all the way through. To complete the cut, hold the sheet and bump the back side with your knee to snap the gypsum. Slice the paper back with a knife.

tips 'n' tricks

Never apply paint or wallpaper directly over paneling. The irregularity of the paneled surface will show through. If you're planning on installing wallpaper, either cover the paneling with a special liner paper called "blank stock" or install ¼-inch drywall over the paneling. If you're painting, either fill the irregularities with drywall compound and sand the surface smooth, or install drywall first.

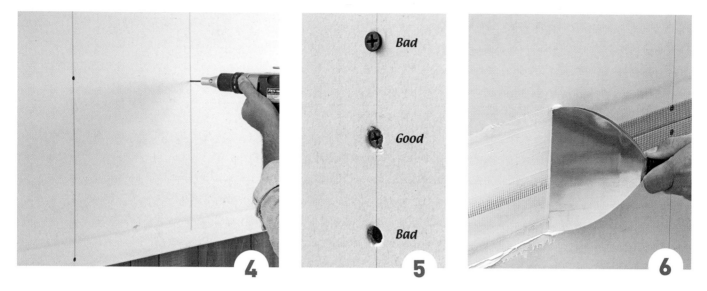

3. Just before you start hanging a sheet, run a heavy bead of caulk around the top and corners of the wall. This step secures the edges of the drywall and fills any air pockets around the perimeter of the sheet.

4. With a helper, lift each sheet in place. Handle the sheets carefully; they are heavy and awkward and can break. Drive screws or nails through the sheet into the wall studs. Begin in the center of a panel and work outward. Space nails or screws about 12 inches apart.

5. Set screw or nail heads just below the surface of the panel, creating a slight dimple, but do not break through the paper facing. If a screw head does break through the paper, place another screw right next to it.

6. To finish the wall, start by filling screw or nail dimples with joint compound, using a 6-inch broad knife. Cover the joints with self-adhesive fiberglass mesh tape; then cover the tape with a coat of drywall compound. Let the first coat dry 24 hours, scrap off ridges and globs, and apply a second coat with a 10-inch knife. Let it dry and apply a third coat, feathering out the edges of the compound. Smooth the surface by sponging or sanding. Sanding creates lots of dust; be sure to wear a mask and eye protection.

tips 'n' tricks

To mark the location of electrical boxes, drive 2- or 3-inch finishing nails into the studs near the top and bottom of the box. Allow the nailheads to protrude about 1 inch above the surface. Position the new sheet of drywall and press it against the wall. The protruding nail heads will indent the back side of the new drywall and mark placement for the cutouts for the switch boxes.

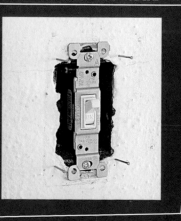

Goodbye to OLD PAINT

If the paint job you want to cover is in good condition, it might require nothing more than a good cleaning and a bit of scraping or patching. But if the paint is chipping and peeling, especially on woodwork, you're better off stripping the old paint down to the wood. This is also true if the area is damaged or if you are going to change to a different finish, such as latex instead of oil-based paint.

Chemical paint removers can handle several layers of stubborn paint in one application. Fortunately several new products on the market make this technique faster, easier, and safer than it was 10 years ago. Still, be sure to protect yourself while working: Wear safety goggles, latex gloves, long sleeves, and a dust mask or respirator. Check for lead paint before beginning work (see page 73).

The least aggressive and easiest product to work with is a water-and-citrus-based stripper, such as CitraStrip, that is nontoxic, low-odor, and environmentally friendly. It works well but it takes a lot more time to be effective, and it can raise the grain of the wood. This might require additionally sanding and prepping.

When a water-based alkaline or lye-based stripper, such as Ready-Strip, is applied, it forms a rubbery coating over the surface. As the material begins to set up, embed the mesh cloth that comes in the kit. When these warm strippers have finished acting on the surface, you can peel away the stripper, and the old surface comes off with it. These strippers are less messy to use and can remove multiple layers of paint.

Oil- or solvent-based strippers are hot strippers. This means you should have no direct contact with these chemicals because they are petroleum-based. Plus you need to ventilate well because of the fumes. These strippers are flammable, volatile, and environmentally damaging, but they work quickly and thoroughly, and do not raise the grain of wood as much as water-based products.

wizard WARNING

In the cauldron of chemicals, paint strippers are among the most caustic. Take extra precautions to create a strong barrier against these chemicals. First, put on a pair of surgical gloves, then wet your gloved hands with water or rub on a light coat of petroleum jelly. Slip a second pair of gloves over the first. Follow the paint remover manufacturer's directions for use, and always work in a well-ventilated area.

To remove paint with a chemical stripper, follow these steps:

1. Working in 1-foot-square sections and using a disposable paintbrush, brush a thick coat of stripper in one direction over the painted surface (see photo on previous page). Do not brush back and forth—this will reduce the chemical's effectiveness. Let the stripper stand for the recommended time, plus 10 minutes, allowing the paint to soften so it can be easily removed. Apply another coat if the first one dries out.

2. Gently scrape away as much of the softened paint as possible with a coarse abrasive pad, a putty knife, or a nylon pot scrubber. Clean the abrasive pad when it becomes clogged, using paint thinner for oil-based strippers and water for water-based strippers.

3. Rub the cleaned surface with a fine abrasive pad and denatured alcohol to remove the last bits of paint and neutralize the surface. Rub with the grain of the wood. Let dry for at least 24 hours.

wizard WARNING

Do not use cotton or terry-cloth towels with hot solvents such as lacquers or thinners. Here's a true story about a friend who was refinishing furniture with an oil-based paint remover, working in his garage. At the end of the day, he hung his oil-soaked rags outside. Three days later he wadded up the now-dry rags and threw them in a plastic trash can in his garage. At 4 o'clock the next morning, my wife and I awoke to the sound of sirens. We looked out and saw that his garage and half his home were on fire. The rags ignited spontaneously. Use nonflammable shop rags. See page 166 for proper disposal methods.

wizard WARNING

Lead and asbestos can be poisonous. Any home built before 1970 probably has materials in it that contain asbestos, and paint applied as recently as 1978 could contain lead. You may need to call a professional contractor to stabilize or remove these materials.

LEAD

The older the paint, the more likely it contains lead. Years ago almost all paint included lead. With the development of latex paints, the use of lead-content paints declined from the 1950s until lead limits were set for all paints in 1978. Dust and chips from damaged or degraded lead paint can contaminate your house and cause serious health problems for you and your family. For safety, any lead-bearing paint in your home that's loose, chipped, or breaking down should be professionally abated.

ASBESTOS

Asbestos has been linked to a number of serious lung diseases. Any home built before 1970 probably contains building materials made with asbestos—anything from sheet flooring to textured ceiling sprays. If these materials are in good condition, they are generally not a threat. The problem with asbestos occurs when the fibers are disturbed and released into the air.

You can cover an asbestos-containing surface, such as a textured ceiling, with new wallboard or skim-coat it with wallboard compound. Don't try to scrape off the texture material. If you want to remove it—or any material containing asbestos—hire an asbestos abatement contractor to take it off and dispose of it safely.

Test sticks, available at home centers and paint stores, reveal the presence of lead in paint. The tip turns red when rubbed over paint that contains lead. Follow the manufacturer's instructions.

CAULK Is King

The secret to sharp, clean, neatly masked paint edges and to perfectly trimmed wallpaper is not in the cutting—it's in the caulking. Before I paint, faux finish, or apply wallpaper to any room, I always caulk the entire room along baseboards and around window and door trim with a white water-based acrylic caulk. I even caulk inside corners.

There are several reasons to do this. First, it can help make your home more energy efficient if any air is leaking through the cracks. Second, the caulk eliminates gaps, giving the room a more finished look, no matter what decorating technique you plan to apply to the room. Finally—and this is why I caulk even where there are no gaps or air leakages—the caulk makes it much easier to make a clean masking line for painting, or a clean cut when trimming wallpaper after application. Acrylic latex caulk, especially, lends resilience to the surface, allowing your trimming knife's blade to glide along easily and stay sharp longer than if you were trying to cut against wood, plaster, or drywall. The result is a neat, precise, almost effortless cut that more than repays the few minutes it takes to apply the caulk. When you open the caulk tube, cut the tip at an angle at the mark for a small bead (photo above right).

cool tool

Caulking is a pretty easy task, and it makes a huge difference when you trim your wallpaper. But it's also a job that typically involves some drips—of caulk, that is. The problem is that most caulking guns don't know when to stop pushing caulk out of the tube, so when you reach the end of a seam, the caulk just keeps coming, leaving a big blob in the corner or dripping all over the floor. Save yourself some cleanup by buying a dripless caulking gun: As soon as you release pressure on the trigger, the caulk stops—right where you want it to.

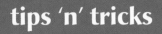

"Caulking is one of the easiest, most satisfying pieces of prep work you'll do."

The trick is to squeeze the caulking gun's trigger evenly while moving the tip of the caulk tube smoothly and at a constant speed. Pull the gun toward the uncaulked part of the gap, leaving a smooth bead of caulking material trailing from the tip of the tube (left and opposite page). Don't stop to smooth the bead while you're laying down caulk—keep going until you reach the end of the gap. Then go back over the gap with a damp sponge, if necessary, to remove any globs or wobbles (left). Keep a bucket of water handy and rinse the sponge continually to prevent caulk from building up on the sponge and smearing onto the wall. Allow to dry overnight.

SEALERS and PRIMERS

Sealers seal, primers prepare surfaces, and sizers restrict porosity. It's not enough to clean walls before you paint or apply wallpaper over them. You also have to seal surfaces that have never been painted. Sealers and primers also provide tooth, a slightly roughened surface to which topcoats of paint and wallpaper can bond.

Sealers

Sealer, also called undercoater, is a prep coat that forms a barrier against moisture and isolates problem areas such as those plagued by mold, stains, or discoloration. Sealers are also used on brand-new walls in baths, kitchens, and other high-moisture areas to help paint and wallpaper bond well. Sealers also allow wallpaper to be easily stripped off later if desired. Sealer products include white-pigmented shellacs and oil-based undercoats. Apply a sealer in two thin coats, sanding lightly—and I do mean lightly—between coats with 220-grit sandpaper. You want to scratch the surface just enough to allow for a good bond. If you're creating a lot of dust, you're sanding way too much.

Primers

Clear primers are used to cover painted walls before applying wallpaper. These products bond to even glossy paint surfaces while giving the wallpaper adhesive a good bonding surface.

They're generally acrylic, water-based products, so they're a bit easier to use than sealers and tend to dry faster.

Sizers

Sizers are used less frequently these days because they're designed for use on plaster, and most walls nowadays are drywall. A sizer is actually a dilution of wallpaper adhesive that's designed to temper the porosity of a plaster wall. Raw plaster is so porous that it can literally absorb all the wallpaper adhesive, leaving nothing on the surface of the wall to hold the wallpaper on. If you've patched a plaster wall, use a sizer on the patched area to assure good adhesion.

wizard WARNING

"Those reality decorating shows never show people washing walls," you say. "Why should I?"

Good question. But do not take lessons in process from what you see on entertainment television. As a wallpapering contractor, I'd be quickly out of business if I did things the way you see them done on those reality decorating shows: no prepping the room, no cleaning the walls, people doing five things to a room at a time—trust me, these shows are entertainment, not instruction. There's simply no substitute for following the steps. Rush things, and the result is a mess. Skipping preparation may make a TV show better, but not your living room walls.

Masking

This last prep step, covering exposed surfaces to protect from splatters and spills, makes painting and wallpapering faster and easier. Think of masking systems as an inexpensive insurance policy that protects you from messy mistakes.

Painting and faux finishing are messy processes

Paint can drip and splatter. It's especially likely to become airborne during some of the more active faux techniques, such as flogging or whacking. In such cases, your tool will hit the adjoining surfaces—it has to for a continuous effect. So you risk producing wide-ranging, multicolor paint splatters that can be very difficult to clean or touch up. For example, if you get blue glaze on an absorbent white popcorn ceiling, the only solution is to repaint the whole ceiling. Wallpaper adhesive can be similarly troublesome. The obvious alternative is good masking.

Masking isn't fun

Everybody hates it. Pros hate it, especially, because we do it so often and because we enjoy creating the finish—not prepping the room. But we do it, and do it meticulously, because we've experienced what happens when we don't. The result, we remember, wasn't pretty, or timesaving.

Plus the pros know that once the preparation is done, we can concentrate fully on creating the desired decorating effect, without having to worry about drips, splatters, and misplaced paint or wallpaper adhesive. Here's how we do it:

- Dispense masking tape in as long a continuous strip as possible to prevent the paint from seeping between any gaps.

- Firmly press the edge of the masking tape as close as possible to the corner or line that separates one surface from another. Run a plastic tool quickly along the edge to set and seal the tape to the surface. For greater splatter protection, leave the tape sticking out away from the surface.

- Masking film is a powerful prevention system. Dispense and cut the film in one continuous strip from corner to corner. Set the tape firmly. Gently unfold the plastic and smooth it to the surface. The film clings to a surface so it won't flip up onto the surface you're working on.

- Wait an hour after painting, then remove the tape and sheeting and dispose of it properly. It is biodegradable, so you can throw it away with your regular trash.

If you are painting the ceiling or sanding a room, this essential step protects walls and woodwork from debris and drips.

1. Firmly press the top edge of blue masking tape along the top of the walls.

2. Slip the edge of the plastic sheeting under the open tape and press the tape down onto the plastic. The sheeting should drape down over the walls and baseboards. This technique can also be used to create a barrier between adjacent rooms to contain dust and fumes to the work area.

Do not remove the sheeting until you are finished with the preparation, painting, and cleanup stages of your project.

quiz the WIZ

How can I keep paint from seeping underneath the edge of masking tape?

The secret to keeping this from happening is to heat-seal the tape. Run a tapered plastic tool quickly over the applied edge of the blue masking tape after you've set the tape. This heats the edge of the tape. The waxy adhesive on the tape melts; when it resolidifies at the edge, it creates a barrier that prevents paint from seeping underneath the tape.

For SAFETY'S Sake

Take every step possible to protect yourself from potential disasters. Here are some reminders:

- **Shut off the power** at the circuit breaker for the room you are painting.

- **Follow the manufacturer's instructions** and safety precautions for all products.

- **Keep paint products out** of the reach of children.

- **Protect your eyes** by wearing safety glasses or goggles when working overhead, using strong chemicals that may splash, or creating or cleaning up dust. Wearing a full-face shield is also a good idea when working overhead or with solvents.

- **Turn off all sources of flame,** including pilot lights, when using any solvent-based compound or paint.

- **Secure all scaffold planks.** Extend the plank 1 foot beyond a support at each end and clamp or nail it into place. Do not step on the plank between its support and its end.

- **Create a proper, secure storage area** where you can keep materials and tools, especially sharp ones, when not in use.

- **Don't work with solvent-based chemicals** if you are pregnant or have heart or lung problems.

- **Rinse oil- or solvent-soaked rags** and spread them out to dry—don't wad them up. Dispose of them carefully. If you want to reuse rags, launder them thoroughly and spread them out to air-dry.

- **Open the legs of a stepladder fully,** lock the leg braces, and make sure the ladder sits level and steady on the floor.

- **Never stand on the top step** of a stepladder, its braces, or work shelf.

- **Never let small children near open containers.** Always cover a 5-gallon bucket with a snap-down lid.

- **Step down and move** the ladder instead of reaching or stretching.

- **Position an extension ladder** so the distance between its feet and the wall it leans against is one-fourth of the ladder's height. Most extension ladders have a sticker on the side showing the proper leaning angle.

- **Check the manufacturer's label** on your ladder to make sure that it can support your weight plus the weight of the tools or materials you will carry up it.

- **Use a scaffold on stairs.** Place an extension plank on the stairway step and a step of the ladder; make sure it is level. Or use a multiladder in its stair scaffolding mode.

- **Create a flow of fresh air** through the room to prevent fumes from building up. Put a box fan in the doorway or window.

tips 'n' tricks

Mixing paint yourself can be messy. Here's how to prevent paint splattering as you mix it with a power drill and attachment. Poke the mixer shaft through a paper plate, then hold the plate against the open top of the can while mixing.

Some preparation tips are summarized here for easy reference.

Preparing to Paint

Paint a piece of white 24x30-inch foam-core board the desired color. When it's dry, use it to test the paint in a variety of light conditions and locations. Hold it vertically on the walls to view it. This method also lets you see how furniture and accessories in a room look when positioned against or next to a particular color.

When patching white walls and molding, mix two drops of red food coloring into every 6 ounces of patching compound to make it easy to spot repairs for sanding later.

Colored party toothpicks make it a snap to remount drapery hardware, towel bars, or picture hooks in a room. Pack toothpicks snugly into each hole you want to reuse. Then spackle the holes without picks. The toothpicks make the holes easy to find when it's time to reattach the hardware.

Never begin a paint project in the public rooms in your home, such as the kitchen, dining room, living room, or any other rooms frequented by guests. Instead try out your colors and build your skill level in a laundry room, bathroom, or bedroom. Even a storage room or garage is a good place to experiment.

Plastic wrap works magic. Use it to cover doorknobs and keep splatters off hardware. If you are painting the ceiling, press a sheet of plastic wrap over your eyeglasses. You can still see through them, but the wrap protects the lenses from paint drops.

Here's a Wall Wizard solution for cleanup: baby wipes. See page 29.

As you disassemble the room, drop all the switch plates into one medium plastic bag. Remount screws back into their fixtures so they don't get lost or scratch the plastic plates. Separate the hardware for each window, door, and curtain into its own bag and mark its location in the room. Once all the hardware has been bagged and tagged, place the bags into one large bag with the room name on it. For safe keeping, stick the bag on the windowpane of the room with blue tape.

Make a trash bag apron from a 13-gallon tall kitchen plastic trash bag. See page 26.

Instead of spending hours masking off window glass, rub lip balm around the inside of each pane.

When the paint dries, take a knife and score around the glass, then scrape the paint and wax away. If you still have wax on the glass, heat the glass with a hair dryer and buff clean.

What can I do about that awful paneling in my living room? My advice is to install ¼-inch drywall over the paneling to gain a clean, fresh surface. If you do want to paint or paper over paneling, you must fill, sand, and prime; or cover the paneling with special liner paper. See pages 69–70.

Think your walls are grime-free? Try this test: Spray a tissue with water and lightly rub it on the wall. See that brown smudge? It's body oils, hair spray, and food oils that become airborne while cooking and eventually settle on the walls. Lots of paint jobs fail because new, clean paint is applied on top of dingy, dirty surfaces. Clean before you paint.

Heard the one about using toothpaste to fill holes in the wall? Here's the real story: Toothpaste doesn't hold up and may contain bleaches that will stain any paint or wallpaper applied over it.

Remove wallpaper with this Secret Stripping Solution:

3 gallons hot water

22 ounces wallpaper remover concentrate

¼ cup liquid fabric softener

1 cup white vinegar

2 tablespoons baking soda

Thinking about painting over wallpaper? Think again! Wallpaper patterns and seam lines can show through the paint. Plus the paint can act as a solvent to the wallpaper paste, causing the paper to fall off the wall while you're painting or bubble, wrinkle, and release irregularly over time.

Any adhesive left on the wall can crackle the paint and prevent it from sticking successfully. To make sure you have removed all the adhesive, give the wall an iodine test. Mix 1 ounce of iodine with 1 quart of water. Use a trigger spray bottle to mist the wall. If the spray on the wall turns bluish purple, adhesive is still there and you need to continue cleaning.

To keep paint from seeping under the edge of masking tape, heat-seal the tape. Run the end of a tapered plastic tool quickly over the applied edge of the blue masking tape after you've set the tape. This heats the edge of the tape, and the waxy adhesive on the tape melts.

chapter 4

Painting

Paint is the first material you apply when redecorating—even if your plan also includes faux finishing and applying wallpaper. That's because basic painting sets the stage for more involved techniques, proving the background or "host" surfaces for more elaborate elements to build upon. Paint is also likely to cover more surface area than any other technique, so it makes sense to apply it first. Finally, the skills you practice in laying down a great painted finish—controlling your material, creating a good working rhythm, working with a partner, and keeping a clean, orderly, organized work area—will be invaluable to you as you move on to more complex techniques.

Wall Wizards are made, not born. I've become a master painter through decades of experience. It takes planning, practice, and patience to become a Wall Wizard. Some techniques come fairly quickly. Others are more challenging—but still manageable.

Tennis players don't start their careers by playing international tournaments at Wimbledon. First, they practice in private. So don't tackle your showpiece entry hall the first time you open a paint can. You'll make mistakes, just as I did.

But in your case, you have the benefit of my experience. As we go along, I'll share tips and techniques that I've learned along the way that'll make your experience as a painter easier and faster than mine. Practice these techniques in a walk-in closet, utility room, or laundry room to start—you'll be less nervous about the results, and more tolerant of an occasional flaw. By the time you get to the public spaces in your home, you'll be ready to create a showpiece.

If your earliest attempts don't live up to your expectations, what have you risked? A can of paint! If you don't like the results the first time, you can always paint over your mistakes. And at an average of about $28 per gallon, paint lets you transform a room for about $100—easily your best decorating value.

In this chapter, we'll focus on two things: managing the material, and knowing how to choose and use the tools of the trade. Ready?

Lets get started!

Formulas for SUCCESS

Finally you've made your decision; you're going to paint your bedroom pale blue. You have several options to find just the right blue:

Standard factory finish

When you choose a gallon of paint straight off the shelf of your home supply store, you have selected a premixed, standard factory finish. Color selection is limited, but because this paint was manufactured in large batches, there are some advantages: Compared to custom-mixed colors, factory-blended paints are mixed more thoroughly, are more resistant to fading, and are more consistent in color.

Standard-mixed colors

You'll find these colors on the paint chip cards displayed in the store. They are mixed in the store according to the paint company's predetermined formula. Most people use these colors for their painting projects.

Custom-mixed colors

Do you want to match your paint color to the small red flowers in your Oriental rug? Then ask for paint custom-mixed by retail paint dealers, decorating centers, or hardware stores. The dealer can perform a computerized analysis of a color card or fabric swatch to determine a precise color formula. This technology makes it easy to mix virtually any color you choose.

Accent colors

Accent colors are factory-prepared, pure, solid colors such as red, blue, yellow, and black. Mix them with each other to get rich, deep colors. Considered premium coatings, they are very durable and resist fading—useful for a sunny room. Used in small, intense ways, they create more drama.

Specialty paints

One other type of paint is worth mentioning here: specialty paint, such as glazes; crackle, suede, and pebble finishes; Venetian plaster; chalkboard paint; and many others. Once available only to professional painters, now they are offered to do-it-yourselfers. I'll talk more about these paints in chapter 5, "Faux Finishing."

Making the GRADE

A Wall Wizard is frugal but never cheap—that's why you should always invest in the best tools and materials you can afford. When it comes to paint, you get what you pay for, and if you pay for less, you'll get less coverage and lower quality results. It's easy to get confused in the store because there are so many different brands to choose from, each with a variety of additives and enhancers. But in reality, there are only three grades of interior paint.

Low grade

The name says it all: Low grade means low price means low coverage. It contains less durable binders, and it uses clays and other inert ingredients to provide coverage. This type is often referred to as professional-grade or architectural-grade paint. Low-grade paint is requested for commercial jobs—in offices or apartments—where frequent repainting is standard maintenance.

Medium grade

A medium-grade paint, also called decorator grade, contains a range of pigments and binders like those used in the premium (high) grade. Medium grade is slightly less expensive than a premium grade.

This kind of paint is an effective substitute for high-grade paint when cost is a factor. Medium-grade paint can be a good choice when you expect to repaint every few years, such as when you redecorate children's rooms. It is also a good choice for low-traffic rooms such as guest rooms or those where there is little wear and tear.

quiz the WIZ

How can I tell what kind of paint is on my walls?

Scrub a small out-of-sight area with detergent, rinse, and towel dry. Using a cotton ball soaked in ammonia, lightly rub the spot. If the paint comes off, it's latex. If not, it's oil-based.

High grade

When you buy the best, you won't be disappointed. High-grade paint is the most expensive type because of the added pigments and binders. It contains the most solid content of the three—up to 45 percent of the contents.

That doesn't mean that your paint job will increase in price just because you use high-grade paint. Compared with a low-grade interior paint, a high-grade paint will spread more easily, splatter less, and show fewer brush marks. Also, because it contains more pigment, it hides flaws better. In the long run, a high-grade paint can actually reduce the cost of your project because it frequently requires the use of only one coat—a coat that, once dry, has a film that is 50 percent thicker than that of a low-grade paint. The result is a tougher, more durable finish that resists fading, yellowing, staining, and abrasion. These paints are more likely to be scrubbable too.

Many paints marketed at premium prices under designers' names offer special surface textures or effects that can enhance a room. Linen and other fabrics, stone, and other finishes are available in special colors. Some of these paints require special preparation or tools; all call for careful application in accordance with the manufacturer's instructions to achieve the full effect. Durability varies; ask your paint dealer whether the special paint you choose will stand up to your intended use.

quiz the WIZ
Which paint is the best?

The best paint balances price and performance, and it should suit the project. You can use low-grade materials when it is applicable, such as for a rental property. On the other hand, high-grade paint is suitable if you don't want to paint as often. Your best bet is to thumb through consumer magazines that test materials on a nonbiased basis.

What's YOUR TYPE?

There are two types of paint: latex and oil-based.

Latex paint

My wife is the love of my life, but latex, or water-based paint, is a close second. It is versatile and easy to use; it dries quickly and cleans up with water. It is nonflammable, almost odor-free, and resists fading, cracking, and chalking. A high-quality latex paint has 100 percent acrylic resin as its binder, while a low-quality latex paint has 100 percent vinyl resin. The latter decreases the durability of the paint. A top-quality latex paint has excellent adhesion to a variety of surfaces.

Oil-based paint

Oil-based paint dries to a water-tight, impervious film. It goes on smoothly; its colors are deep and saturated. The film is extremely durable and has a greater resistance to fading in sunlight. But, oil-based paints can sag during application, they take longer to dry and turn yellow with age. They can also seal moisture into wood that's not completely dry, causing it to rot. If surfaces are not properly prepared, oil-based paint can crack and discolor. Oil-based materials and solvents are bad for the environment: The fumes of their solvents degrade air quality, and both paints and solvents contaminate groundwater if not disposed of properly. Cleanup is more complicated than for latex paints.

Latex paints offer many advantages over oil-based paints, including ease of application and cleanup, durability, versatility, and low impact on the environment.

tips 'n' tricks

Water-based paint won't stick to oil paint, so if you want to apply latex paint over a previous oil-based finish, here's what to do: First, clean the surface thoroughly with rubbing alcohol on a scrub sponge. Wipe the surface with a cloth saturated with rubbing alcohol and let dry. Repair and fill any damage to the surface. Apply two thin coats of oil-based primer-sealer, such as Kilz, to give the latex paint a surface it can adhere to. Using an oil-based paint over latex does not require any special preparation.

Behind the SHEENS

Sheen describes the degree of light reflection off the painted surface—in other words, how the paint shines.

Sheen affects the finish's appearance, durability, and suitability for certain uses. As the amount of sheen increases, so does the enamel value, which determines the hardness or protective value of the coating. Manufacturers use many names to describe the different paint sheens, such as eggshell. Because sheens are not standardized, one manufacturer's satin or semigloss paint can have more shine than that of another. Here are the most common finishes:

Flat paint has the least amount of shine because it has a nonreflective matte finish. The matte finish hides surface imperfections, but tends to absorb moisture and allow dirt to stick to it, so it can get dingy more quickly and be more difficult to clean than glossier finishes.

Satin paint, also known as eggshell, has a soft luster. It still has some texture, but it's more impervious to moisture than flat paint, so it's more resistant to dirt and staining and is easier to clean.

Semigloss paint has a higher sheen than satin paint. The light-reflective quality of a semigloss can highlight surface imperfections and cause distracting reflections, so it is generally not a good choice for imperfect surfaces. It is, however, an excellent choice for woodwork, doors, and windows, because it tends to stay cleaner and stands up to scrubbing if necessary.

Gloss paint is the most durable, stain-resistant, and easiest to clean. Its hard, shiny surface is tougher and hides brush strokes. Glossy colors are intense, a characteristic that can highlight surface imperfections and overpower a room if used for walls. It is an excellent choice for woodwork, however, especially in areas exposed to heavy traffic, such as kitchen and bathroom walls, banisters, railings, and cabinets.

cool tool

Recently, a new paint became available that is as impervious to moisture as a semigloss or gloss paint, but with the soft, nonreflective surface of a traditional flat paint. Known as "scrubbable flat" paints, these new formulations offer the best of both worlds, giving you a wider range of sheen options, even for wear- and dirt-prone areas. I love the stuff!

HOW MUCH PAINT?

Too much or just the right amount? That's the question when trying to figure out how much paint to purchase. It is handy to have a little extra paint on hand for touch-ups, but who wants to spend the money and be stuck with more paint than you need?

If you're not a numbers person, the following steps may sound like gibberish. Just take it slow and break out each step—at the end you'll arrive at an accurate estimate for the amount of paint you need.

1. Calculate the square footage of the surfaces to be painted. Measure the length and width of the room and determine its perimeter, which is the distance all around the room. For example, if the room is 13 feet wide and 18 feet long, its perimeter is 62 feet (13 feet + 13 feet + 18 feet + 18 feet).

2. Multiply the perimeter by the room's height to get the square footage of wall space. If the room is 8 feet high, then its square footage is 496 square feet (62 feet × 8 feet).

3. Count the doors and windows in the room. Subtract from your wall area 21 square feet for each standard door and 15 square feet for each standard window. (If your room has large doors, such as a sliding patio door, or large windows, you can measure the width and height of each door and window, then figure the exact square footage of each. You don't need to be precise; round to the nearest square foot.) The room in the example has one standard door and three standard windows, so subtract 66 square feet (21 square feet + 3 × 15 square feet) from the wall area. The answer is the amount of wall area to be painted: 430 square feet (496 square feet – 66 square feet).

4. To find the number of gallons of paint needed, divide the wall area by 300—the square footage easily covered by a gallon of interior paint. In the example, you would need a little more than 1.4 gallons to paint the walls; round that up to 1½ gallons—one gallon and two quarts.

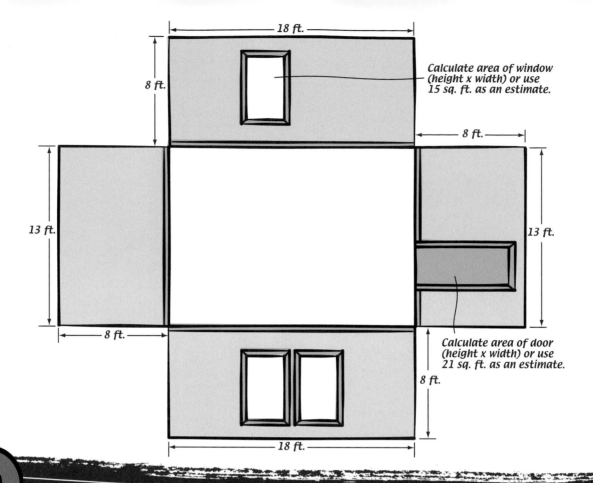

18 ft.

8 ft.

Calculate area of window (height x width) or use 15 sq. ft. as an estimate.

8 ft.

13 ft.

13 ft.

8 ft.

Calculate area of door (height x width) or use 21 sq. ft. as an estimate.

8 ft.

18 ft.

tips 'n' tricks

After that lesson in estimating, you'll be relieved to learn these tried-and-true Wall Wizard tricks.

- A gallon of paint will cover about 300 square feet of wall area. Some manufacturers stretch it to 400 square feet, but go with the lesser amount to keep from running out of paint in the middle of a job.

- Always buy more paint than you need. This extra amount allows for spillage, waste, and spots that soak up more paint than expected. Plaster, for example, is more absorbent than wallboard. Also, you'll want leftover paint for future touch-ups. Remember to buy extra paint if you plan to paint the interiors of built-in bookshelves or cabinets.

- Another reason to buy more paint? Custom-mixed colors vary slightly from batch to batch, so it's best to buy enough paint at one time instead of running out and having to match the colors.

- If you can't decide between 4 or 5 gallons, go with 5 and buy it in a 5-gallon container. It should actually be cheaper than three 1-gallon cans, and you're guaranteed the color will be the same.

PREPPING Paint

Take the time to box, strain, and condition your paint before you use it, and you'll be rewarded with easier application, more consistent results, and a higher-quality, longer-lasting finish.

Boxing

If you have several cans to use for a job, the color can vary from can to can. Ensure a uniform color by mixing all the paint together, a technique known as *boxing*.

Pour all the paint into a clean plastic 5-gallon bucket. Mix it until it is uniform in color. Pour the boxed paint back into the cans. Tightly seal the lids on all but the can you're ready to use.

Straining

Straining eliminates lumps in the paint. If the paint has separated, stir the thick paint up from the bottom of each can to free as many lumps as possible. Then box the paint, pouring it all together through a nylon paint strainer and into the bucket.

Paint less than one year old usually doesn't require straining. Older paint might have a thick skin on the top; remove the skin and set it aside. Box the paint, pouring it through a nylon paint strainer into the bucket. When the skin has dried, wrap it in newspaper and discard.

Conditioning

Paint stored for a year or longer may need conditioner to improve its flow, adhesion, and coverage. New paint can be conditioned too. The conditioner adds elasticity and retards drying, making it easier to maintain a wet edge during painting—important for reducing overlap marks. I use paint conditioner on almost every job I do.

Following the manufacturer's instructions, add a conditioner such as Floetrol to water-based paint or Penetrol to oil-based paint.

The THREE LAWS of PAINTING

It's time to lay down the law—the three immutable laws of painting. These are the secrets of painting. Use them to control the paint in its liquid state. Understanding and utilizing these laws dictates the way you apply paint. To be a Wall Wizard, you have to master the medium, so it does not master you.

 ## Never paint out of a paint can.

- **Container contamination.** As you paint, your brush picks up dust, grease, grime, fly boogers, spider snots, and other spots. When you dip into the can to reload, all that debris ends up back in the can, contaminating the paint. That causes flecks and specks in the paint finish.

- **Dangerous drying.** If you ever have painted from an open, full can, you probably noticed as you worked that the paint became gooier, stickier, and thicker. This is the air reacting with the exposed paint, which is setting up in the can, not on the wall.

- **Material mover.** A paint can is strictly a storage and delivery container. It was never designed to be painted from or carried around; it's too awkward and heavy. You are more likely to knock it over and spill, especially the gallon size.

2 Pour no more than ½ inch of paint into the container.

- **Material management.** Pour only ½ inch of paint into a plastic bucket to stage and control it before application. This forces you to refresh the paint more often, keeping it in its liquid state for better flow and bond to the surface.

- **Lighter load.** With only ½ inch of paint in your bucket, you carry less weight, work faster with better control, and avoid fatigue by the end of the job.

- **Spill spoiler.** Because you have only ½ inch of paint in the bucket, if you happen to stumble, the paint is less likely to spill out. And if you do happen to spill, there's less to clean up.

3 The enemy of paint is air.

- **Air wars.** The air around us is the drying agent for paint. Paint doesn't dry in a sealed paint can, but the minute you open the can, air rushes in and starts the drying process. Limiting paint's exposure to air until the paint is where you want it to be is a way of controlling the project.

- **O_2 factor.** In simple terms, oxygen is the reactor that turns paint from a liquid to a solid. Exposure to air thickens the paint, creating drag during the application, producing brushstrokes in the finish.

- **Cap it.** Reduce paint's exposure to air by immediately replacing the lid on the paint can. Cover your working container (bucket or tray). To seal a can for storage, use the techniques described on page 162.

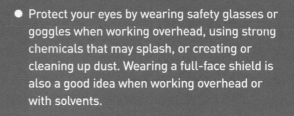

wizard WARNING

It goes without saying that Wall Wizards take proper safety precautions. Always take every step possible to protect yourself from potential disasters. Here are some reminders:

- Shut off the power at the circuit breaker for the room you are painting or wallpapering.

- Follow the manufacturer's instructions and safety precautions for all products.

- Keep paint products out of the reach of children.

- *Keep pets and children away from work areas.*

- Protect your eyes by wearing safety glasses or goggles when working overhead, using strong chemicals that may splash, or creating or cleaning up dust. Wearing a full-face shield is also a good idea when working overhead or with solvents.

- Turn off all sources of flame, including pilot lights, when spraying any solvent-based compound or paint.

- Secure all scaffold planks. Extend the plank 1 foot beyond a support at each end and clamp or nail it into place. Do not step on the plank between its support and its end.

- Create a proper, secure storage area where you can keep materials and tools, especially sharp ones, when not in use.

- *Check the manufacturer's label on your ladder to make sure that it can support your weight plus the weight of the tools or materials you will carry up it.*

● *Use a scaffold on stairs. Place an extension plank on the stairway step and a step of the ladder; make sure it is level.*

● Step down and move the ladder instead of stretching.

● Position an extension ladder so the distance between its feet and the wall it leans against is one-fourth of the ladder's height. Most extension ladders have a sticker on the side showing the proper leaning angle.

● Follow the manufacturer's instructions when you operate power painting equipment.

● Don't work with solvent-based chemicals if you are pregnant or have heart or lung problems.

● Rinse oil- or solvent-soaked rags and spread them out to dry—don't wad them up. Dispose of them carefully. If you want to reuse rags, launder them thoroughly and spread them out to air-dry.

● Open the legs of a stepladder fully, lock the leg braces, and make sure the ladder sits level and steady on the floor.

● Never stand on the top step of a stepladder, its braces, or its work shelf.

● Never let small children near open containers. Always cover a 5-gallon bucket with a snap-down lid.

● *Create a flow of fresh air through the room to prevent fumes from building up. Put a box fan in the doorway or window.*

BASIC Painting 101

Because the paint finish is only as good as the surface to which it's applied, start your project by cleaning, repairing, and preparing all the surfaces in the room. Here are the practical methods and techniques for applying finish coats on the most common interior surfaces.

Break your work down into logical steps and procedures. Don't rush; set plenty of time aside for each task. Think safety; most accidents result from lack of awareness and overestimating your abilities. In general, work down and out of the room; start with the ceiling, then walls, then floors. This concept will provide you a consistent starting and ending point. The best wall to start on is the door wall, so your skills are honed by the time you reach the more visible surfaces across from the entrance.

Complete tasks, don't skip around from project to project, stay focused, and follow the procedures and techniques for the best results. Drying takes time. Don't rush the paint; allow enough time between coats for best results. And finally, RELAX! Enjoy the process; the results will be worth your time and effort. It will give you a sense of accomplishment, satisfaction, and success.

tips 'n' tricks

Here's a great control concept: Line your paint pot with a large resealable bag. Open the mouth of the bag and pull down over the edge of the bucket rim. Secure with a large rubber band. Now, if you need to pause from painting the bag can be closed to prevent drying. If you need to change colors, drop in a new bag. Cleanup is a snap—just throw the used bag away.

5

6

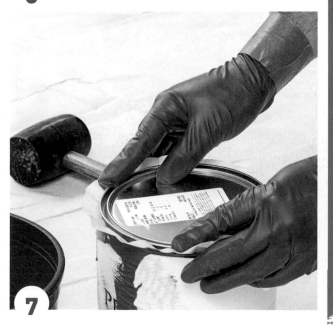

7

Opening act

Your opening moment has arrived—pry open a can of paint.

1. Use a 10-in-1 tool to gently open the paint can. Do not use a screwdriver; it will bend and distort the lid shape.

2. Dab a spot of the paint on the side of the can and the lid to identify the type of paint sheen and color.

3. Slide the wet paint lid into a plastic zip-closure bag. This prevents the paint from drying, stops the lid from dripping paint, and provides a clean lifting tab to be able to open, pour and close the can as needed.

4. Punch holes in the groove inside the rim, called the lid well, with a hammer and nail or with the sharp point of the 10-in-1 tool and a mallet. The holes allow excess paint to drain back into the can. After the project is finished, the lid can set and seal properly because the lid well doesn't fill up with paint, impeding the seal. These drain holes also help prevent spattering when you replace the lid.

5. Lightly stir the paint.

6. Pour only ½ inch of paint into the paint bucket.

7. Be sure to place the lid back on the paint can; remember—the enemy of paint is air.

cool tool

Make a custom paint pot. Take a 2-quart plastic bucket; make a small hole in the side about 2 inches down from the rim. Fasten a 3-inch pot magnet on the inside with a machine bolt, a nylon locknut, and two fender washers. Put duct tape over the magnet. The magnet will hold the brush by its metal ferrule to keep it from sitting on the bottom of the bucket, which would over-load the brush and bend the bristles. Add a flexible handle made from duct tape. Put a short piece, sticky-sides-together, in the middle of a longer piece. Attach the tape to one side of the bucket, around your hand, and up the other side. Remember the tool rule: Make the tool hold you, so you don't have to hold the tool.

BRUSH Works

Handling a brush

A paintbrush is a paint detail tool. Its design is based on the way you use it. It seems simple, but people spend thousands of dollars learning how to hold a golf club, so it's only fitting that you learn the proper way to hold and use a paintbrush.

● Always hold and use your painting tool in your dominant hand. As you work, keep the tool in front of your face; you will have better physical and visual control.

● Hold the brush firmly with your thumb on one side of the ferrule and your fingers spread across the opposite side. You can also grip the brush like a pen or pencil, letting the handle rest comfortably in the hollow where your thumb joins your hand.

● Use long sweeping strokes to apply and spread out the paint. These broader movements will give you better leverage and minimize muscle fatigue.

Typical grip
Grip the brush lightly, with your thumb underneath and your fingers on top of the ferrule. Let the handle rest in the joint where your thumb joins your hand.

wizard WARNING

Take care of yourself! Painting is one of the most repetitive, stressful jobs you can do with your hands. I have carpal tunnel syndrome from all the years I have spent painting. To help avoid the same fate, pay careful attention to what I tell you on this page about how to properly hold and use your tools. You are your most important tool—take care of yourself.

Trim touch
Hold a small trim brush like a pen or pencil, with the handle resting in the hollow of your thumb joint.

Dip, wiggle, and pat: loading a brush

A paintbrush is designed to lay paint on a surface, not to store it. Here's how to control the tool and the paint.

1. **Dip** your brush into the paint. Since you have only ½ inch of paint in your paint pot, you can't overload the brush bristles or force excess paint into the ferrule.

2. **Wiggle** to load paint into the bristle tips. When you wiggle, you open the bristles, allowing the paint to flow into the brush.

3. **Pat** both sides of the brush lightly against the inside of the paint pot as you lift it out. This will release any excess paint from the outside of the brush, where most drips come from. (The paint inside the brush is held there by capillary action.) **Never scrape** your brush on the side of the paint pot. If you do, you'll risk breaking bristles and damaging the tool. You'll also risk scraping dried, caked-on paint from the tops of the bristles and the rim of your paint pot into the liquid paint, where they can contaminate the finish.

Three strokes—you're on!

Gravity is your friend, so work from the bottom of the wall up with strokes about 16 to 24 inches long. Apply the paint in three strokes for a smooth finish:

1. The first stroke is always up to unload the brush.

2. The second stroke is gently down to set the paint onto the surface.

3. The third stroke is up to smooth the paint and remove brush marks.

Overbrushing the paint tends to thin out the finish and makes brush marks more apparent. Also, because the paint immediately starts to dry once it leaves the brush, you're starting to drag thickened, drying paint around, increasing effort and resulting in gobs and streaks in the finish. Instead, apply the paint quickly, moving up and along the wall, painting from bottom to top, moving forward between strokes. While moving at the end of last stroke, lift the brush tip off the surface to "feather" the paint back into your wet paint. This step will help the paint blend evenly onto the surface. After you have laid on a section of paint, make one continuous, final stroke to eliminate the overlapping sections and bristle stroke marks. While the paint is fresh, look for any drips, runs, or bare spots ("holidays"), because now is the only opportunity you'll have to easily fix them. Wizards work wet!

cool tool

A plastic milk jug makes managing paint during a project easy. Cut an opening as illustrated. Stop about 2 inches from the bottom. Cut an inverted V-shaped slit and a diamond-shaped hole near the neck of the jug to hold your brush. To hold it easily, slip your hand into the handle with your palm toward the jug. When finished, pour unused paint back into the can using the jug top as a funnel. Stretch an old nylon stocking over the opening to filter the paint. You can clean and reuse the jug or toss it in the trash.

PAD Works

Handling a paint pad

A pad is the ideal detail paint tool. A little understanding and practice will help you use this high-tech tool to lay paint faster, better, and more evenly on any surface.

- Look for complete paint pad kits. The plastic packaging for the kits is also the loading paint tray and an airtight lid.

- Make the tool hold you: Make a flexible handle. Place the empty tray in your hand, palm side up, then stick a piece of tape down one side of the tray, loosely over the back of your hand, and up the other side.

- Always hold and use your painting tool in your dominant hand. Grip the pad handle firmly as you paint. Keep the tool in front of your face; you will have a better view of your work and better physical control of the tool.

- The tracking wheels—that's what got you interested in this gizmo in the first place, right? You thought they would eliminate having to use masking tape. Wrong. Even though pads are designed to deliver the paint right up to the edge of adjacent surfaces, they are not foolproof. What can easily happen is that when you load the pad, paint gets smeared onto the wheels and they leave little paint marks along the wall or ceiling or trim. Take out some painting insurance—masking tape!

- Load the pad and tray often. This prevents the pad from drying out.

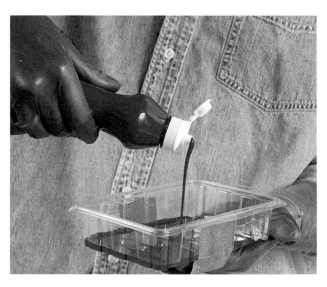

- Use long sweeping strokes to apply and spread out the paint. These broader movements will give you better leverage and minimize muscle fatigue.

- If you need to stop painting for a short time, set and store the pad inside the tray and snap on the lid to stop the paint from drying in the tray.

Dip, wiggle, and scrape: loading a paint pad

A paint pad is designed to evenly load and lay paint to a surface. Don't overwork this tool. Here are some techniques that will give you much better control.

1. **Dip** the pad into the paint. Pour only ¼ inch of paint into the loading tray. This amount won't let you overload the pad bristles, or let the pad sink into the paint, or easily spill the tray.

2. **Wiggle** the pad to load the paint into its bristles and foam core. This action will pump in, load up, and lock in the paint.

3. **Scrape** the pad gently across the edge of the tray. Don't press too hard; you want the bristles to be full of paint, but not dripping. The excess paint will flow back into the paint tray. This lets you control the load amount going onto the surface.

Different strokes

Remember that gravity is your friend, so work from bottom to top and from side to side with strokes about 24 to 36 inches long. You'll need only two strokes for a smooth finish.

1. Place the loaded pad firmly on the surface. The first stroke is always in one direction to unload the paint in the pad.

2. The second stroke runs gently back over the area in the opposite direction to set the paint and remove bristle marks. At the end of this stroke, lift the pad while moving to feather back into the wet paint. This will help the paint blend evenly onto the surface.

Apply the paint quickly, moving up and along the wall, painting from bottom to top, moving forward between strokes.

cool tool

Make a micro paint grid. Cut a rectangle of #14 stainless steel mesh screen slightly larger than the inside dimensions of the paint tray. Measure in ¼ inch from the screen edge and bend the screen down to form the legs of the grid. Place the grid inside the paint tray. It prevents the pad from sinking too deep into the paint and getting paint up into the tracking wheels.

ROLLER Works

A roller cover and roller frame are the perfect tools for painting large surfaces. Screw in an extension pole on the end of the frame for better leverage as you work. Here's the best way to hold, control, and use this simple painting system:

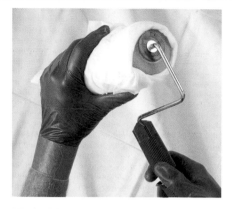

Dip, rake, and roll: loading a roller

Get the tool ready to paint to improve the coverage and quality of your paint job.

1. Start by slightly moistening the roller cover with water (if using latex paint) or paint thinner (if using oil-based paint). After dampening the cover, wrap a clean shop rag around it and blot dry. This pre-dampening helps the tool draw in more paint through capillary action, and will make it easier to clean later.

2. Pour ½ inch of paint into your paint tray (a plastic-lined metal tray) or a bag-lined bucket and loading grid, if you have a lot of painting to do. Fill a paint bucket no more than one-third full. By loading the containers in this way, you keep them light and easy to handle, make them less likely to spill and spatter, and give the paint less exposure to air, as you're refilling the containers more often.

3. Using even strokes, roll the roller down the slope of the tray, called the rake, and gently **dip** the roller cover into the paint well to load the tool. Repeat this two or three times; try not to slosh the roller around. Don't immerse the entire roller; this will overload it. Just dip the roller cover into the paint.

4. Slightly lift the roller directly above the tray and move it back up to the top of the **rake**. **Roll** slowly down the slope of the tray. Repeat this several times to force the paint up into the roller cover and ensure the paint is loaded evenly. Don't spin the roller rapidly; it will splatter the paint. Work the paint deep into the roller. **Keep rolling down the rake** until the roller is evenly coated with paint but not dripping.

cool tool

Have you ever accidentally spilled, stepped in, or knocked over the paint tray? Then you'll love this Wizard tool: Make a paint bucket trolley! Buy a large, round plastic planter base with casters. Get a 5-gallon bucket and a length of 2-inch foam pipe insulation. Cut the bucket off about 10 inches from the bottom. Center the bucket on the plant dolly and attach with screws. Apply the pipe insulation around the rim of the plant mover to make a bumper. Set a painting bucket with loading grid into the cut-off bucket and you're rollin'.

Let's roll

A roller cover and frame is designed to roll paint on a surface; it is not meant to splatter it. Do not overload this tool, and do not roll too quickly. With your paint roller loaded, approach the wall.

1. Hold the roller frame and pole firmly with both hands. Place your dominant hand at the bottom end of the pole for more control. Place your other hand in the middle to act as a leverage point that will mechanically triple the amount of force applied to the roller. As you work, keep the tool in line with your body; you will have better balance, stamina, and vision.

2. Position the roller so that the open end points the direction you are painting. This keeps the roller from sliding off the roller frame.

3. Follow the three-stroke rule:

   ● **The dump.** The first stroke is always up to unload the paint roller. By rolling upward, you can see what we call the "wave" of liquid paint at the intersection of the roller cover and the wall. Adjust your speed and pressure so you don't run out of paint before the end of your stroke, or cause the wave to spill over the ends of the roller and cause drips. Use a long, continuous stroke to apply and spread the paint. Roll from the baseboard all the way up to the ceiling. This long stroke gives you better leverage and reduces muscle fatigue (compared to short, choppy movements), and it gives you more even coverage.

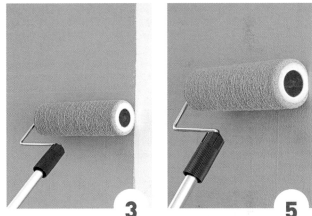

   ● **The set.** The second stroke is straight back down the initial swath to evenly coat the wall, set the paint pigments onto the surface, and aerate the paint to start the drying process. Again, stroke the full height of the surface.

   ● **The lay.** The third stroke is a light upstroke to smooth out or lay-off the paint finish. We call it "laying off," because we use the texture of the roller to give the surface an evenly stippled effect. As you begin your third stroke up, twist the roller extension pole slightly in the direction you are working. This move puts more pressure on the leading end of the roller—the one that hits the unpainted part of the wall first—to deliver maximum paint where it's needed. It also creates less pressure on the trailing end of the roller, the end on the wet side of the paint job. This helps eliminate the ridges of wet paint we call snail trails that are caused by too much roller pressure.

4. Reload the roller, move one roller width over, allowing for a 1-inch overlap. Repeat the dump, set, and lay strokes, and continue working across the wall. Move your paint tray along with you so you don't have to reach or walk around the room to load the roller. I like to keep my roller tray about 2 feet ahead of me—that way I don't have to twist or bend, and I'm not going to step backwards into a tray I can't see.

5. If you're applying semigloss or high gloss paint, such as in a bathroom or kitchen, you'll get a more consistent sheen if you make an additional light, continuous upward stroke from floor to ceiling to even out the paint. Do this after you've finished the initial application of three to four roller widths of paint.

6. Keep moving forward. As with any application tool, keep a wet edge of paint. Remember: Wizards work wet.

CEILING Solutions

Ceilings pose a special challenge to even the most experienced Wall Wizards because you are working upside down. Before you start painting, cover the floor and any remaining furniture or appliances in the room.

Use a 4- to 6-foot telescopic extension pole on your roller frame. This keeps your feet firmly on the ground. It also makes the job go easier and faster because you don't have to move and climb up and down a stepladder. And because you're farther from the roller, you're less likely to get splattered. If you're going to paint a room's ceiling, do so before painting any other surface in the room.

First, remove the light fixture and ceiling fans and mask the appropriate surfaces. Clean and prepare the surface properly. Begin by cutting in about 4 feet, starting from the corner farthest from the room's entry door. It's all right to slightly overlap down onto the wall. This will save you time as you paint the ceiling and walls. Because you will be cutting in around each wall,

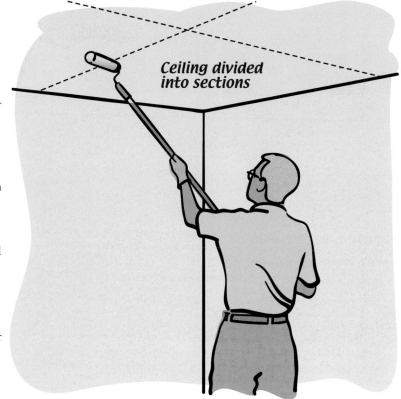

Ceiling divided into sections

the wall paint will cover this overlap. Alternate between cutting-in and rolling-out, working in sections across the ceiling and using the three-stroke method—out, in, out. The last stroke should always be in the same direction as the first to keep the sheen consistent.

quiz the WIZ
Does it matter what the weather is like when I paint?

Yes, weather can make a difference when you are painting. Paint flows and bonds best when the humidity and temperatures are moderate. For most of the country, that means the best time to paint is in late spring or early fall. In a hot, dry environment, paint dries too quickly, before it has a chance to level out, leaving a poor finish quality. In a humid environment, paint takes forever to dry and can sag and droop. If you have to paint in less-than-ideal conditions, use paint conditioner as described earlier in this chapter. In addition, use a humidifier to add some moisture to the air in dry conditions, and a dehumidifier to extract some of the moisture from the air in humid conditions.

My Mistake

CLEAR THE ROOM

Organization is the key to success in anything you do—and that goes double when painting, faux finishing, or wallpapering. Doing a great decorating job is mostly about the process. If you don't have the process down, you're sunk. And for the process to work, you have to clear the room.

Here's how I found out: I was wallpapering a room with a very expensive vase sitting on a credenza. "I can work around that," I thought. After all, I was covering only one wall, and the credenza was positioned well away from the wall I was working on.

Well, I was right—until the last wipe down. I finished it with a flourish and backed up to admire my work—right into the credenza. The vase, of course, toppled to the floor and smashed to smithereens.

Cost of wallpaper job: $300. Cost of vase: $3,000. Net loss: You can do the math; it's too painful for me to calculate. I could just as easily have made the same mistake while painting or faux finishing.

Lesson learned: Always clear the space you're working in before you begin the job. Always have everything put away and covered. Or else.

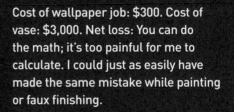

TRIM Works

Architectural embellishments such as crown moldings, doors, baseboards, and window casings are called trim. They are usually constructed of wood, vinyl, or metal. If finished well, these surfaces are what people most admire about a project.

Because trim such as door or window frames can be exposed to wear, thoroughly repair and prepare the surfaces to ensure the paint's bond and finish. Trim work is easy to paint; it just takes a steady hand and the patience to work slowly and methodically. Before you begin, mask all wall surfaces.

Work from the moldings at the top of the wall down to the baseboards to avoid drips on the finish coat you just applied. Use the three-stroke rule for application. If you're right-handed, work from right to left; if you're left-handed, work from left to right. That's because working in these directions allow you to move your body in the direction it naturally wants to go and use your dominant hand.

Always paint with the grain and length of the trim work. Paint horizontal sections with horizontal strokes and vertical sections with vertical strokes. Treat each trim piece as a separate section. Apply the paint quickly. Work each separate trim piece from the bottom up. This helps prevent drips by dragging the paint upward. Keep a wet edge. Wizards work wet: If you let the paint dry, there will be a noticeable transition line in the finish where wet paint overlapped dry paint, causing a double-thick finish. If you maintain a wet edge, the finish will remain even. At the end of last stroke, lift the brush tip off the surface to feather the paint back into the wet paint. This will help the paint blend evenly onto the surface. After you have finished a section of paint, make one continuous, final stroke to eliminate the overlapping sections and bristle marks. Take one final look back over your work to make sure there are no drips or bare-spots ("holidays"). Now is the only chance you'll get to fix it while it's still wet.

tips 'n' tricks

To make your final finish magical, apply two thin coats of paint rather than one heavy coat. Allow the first coat to dry thoroughly, then lightly sand the surface with a 320-grit sandpaper in the direction you are laying on the paint. Clean the surface. Apply the second coat for the finished effect. The first thin coat dries faster and bonds better to the surface. The second coat deepens the color coverage. With one heavy coat, you run the risk of the paint sagging, creating a poor finish quality.

Window work

Casement and sash windows are a big part of trim work. Windows can be tricky to paint, but when you break down the job into steps and stages, it's easier to do. Because windows are exposed to weather, thoroughly prepare them for painting. Repair any mechanical problems to ensure their proper operation.

Remove and store all the hardware so you can clean, prepare, and paint the surface without damaging it. Mask the appropriate surfaces.

Paint the windows at the beginning of the day, so they will be thoroughly dry by the time you want to close them.

Use a combination of rolling and brushing for a beautiful finish. Apply the paint with a 4-inch closed-end foam roller, then stroke out the finish with the paintbrush. This technique allows the roller to deliver the paint quickly and evenly onto the surface, while the brush lays off the finish. Begin applying the paint to the deepest part of the window, working to the shallowest part, and from the farthest outside corner in so you're never reaching over wet paint (see illustrations below). Work in the same direction as the grain.

Apply two coats of paint for the best results. When the finish is thoroughly dry, replace all the hardware.

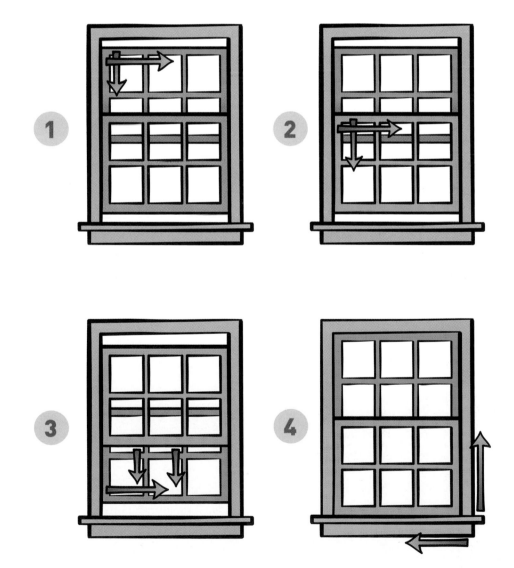

Painting doors

DOOR DETAILS

Doors (including cabinet doors), frames, and casework are all considered trim work. These elements are usually constructed of wood, vinyl, or metal. Because doors are the entrance and exit points, plan to paint them last, so the paint finishes will be undisturbed and allowed to dry upon completion of the room. The easiest way to paint a door is while it is in its frame on its hinges for four reasons:

You preserve its fit and function. If you remove the heaviest part of the system—the door—the frame may shift, and the door may not fit or function properly when replaced.

You avoid damage. If you remove the door, you have to carry it through the house, which means you can damage your walls, moldings, and the door when you move it.

You save time. If you take the door out of its frame and set it on sawhorses, you can only paint one side at a time. You have to wait for one side to dry before you can paint the other, which wastes time.

You end up with a better finish. If you remove a door and take it outside to paint it, you risk getting dust, debris, and bugs in your finish.

Clean the hinges with rubbing alcohol, then mask them with two coats of rubber cement (peel the cement off when finished). Prep the same as window trim. Remove or mask the doorknobs, lock, and other hardware and bag and tag them for easy replacement. Clean the surfaces to be painted with a scrub sponge saturated with rubbing alcohol. The alcohol dissolves all the grease and grime, evaporates without raising the grain like a water-based cleaner would, and lubricates the scrub sponge, effectively wet-sanding the surface, giving the new finish something to adhere to.

For any type of door, start by painting the frame (casing), working up from the inside bottom, across the header, and down the striker side. Don't paint the top or bottom of the door—ever! Leaving those surfaces unpainted allows the door to expand and contract with changes in humidity.

HOW TO PAINT A PLAIN DOOR

To paint a plain door, start by painting the inside hinge edge, working around the door in one direction. Use a combination of rolling and brushing, applying the paint with a 4-inch closed-end foam roller (photo 1). Run two or three roller widths the full height and across the door face, then lay off the finish by brushing from bottom to top with a lightly loaded brush (photo 2). This technique allows the roller to deliver the paint quickly and evenly to the surface while keeping a wet edge and leaves a smooth brush finish.

The same basic technique applies to painting cabinet doors—work from the inside out and the bottom to the top.

HOW TO PAINT A PANELED DOOR

You approach painting a paneled door a bit differently than a plain door. Apply the paint with same roller and brush techniques. Begin by painting each panel, starting with the upper left-hand panel (1) working down the door face in sequence (2, 3, 4). Starting from the bottom of each of the center vertical stiles (5, 6) lay down and brush out the paint. Next, working from the top member (7) down, continue painting each horizontal member (8, 9). Finally, paint the full-height outer stiles (10, 11) and edge (12). Lay-off any runs or sags as you paint.

Allow the paint to dry, lightly sand, and apply the second coat. When the paint is dry, score around the edge of the hinges with a knife and peel away the cement. Replace the hardware.

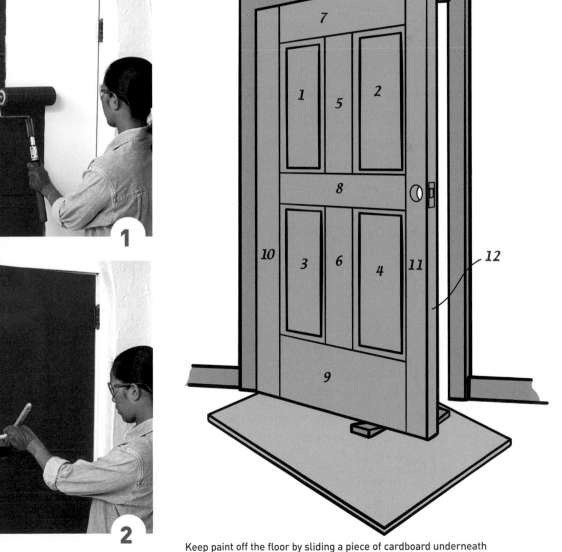

Keep paint off the floor by sliding a piece of cardboard underneath the door. Brace the door with wood shims to hold it steady.

Working a ROOM

It takes two people to effectively paint a room: the cutter person and the roller person.

Choose the right person for the right job. Break down your plan into logical and manageable steps. Identify, define, and divide the workload into separate but equally important tasks. One person uses a brush or a pad to apply a narrow band of paint around the room where one surface meets another. This is called *cutting-in.* The other uses a roller and an extension pole to continuously and consistently apply the paint to large surfaces. This is called *rolling-out.*

If you're detail oriented, handle the cutting-in and trim work. If you're stronger, paint with the roller. Working in a team of two makes the job twice as fast and half as tedious, saving you energy, time, and money.

Stay focused on your assigned task, because the more you do something, the better and faster you become. Your satisfaction level will rise, and your results will look even better.

Direction connection

If you're right-handed, you will find it easier to paint from left to right. If you're left-handed, work from right to left. Begin painting from the corner behind a door or closet. The cutter paints out from a corner, then the roller comes behind and rolls the paint over the wet cut-in band. Continue working around the room this way.

Of course, one person can paint a room working alone, but it takes much longer, and it's harder to keep the paint flowing and maintain a wet edge. If you must work alone, paint in small, manageable sections and work quickly but methodically.

wizard WARNING

Don't cut-in an entire room and then roll out the walls. What happened to maintaining a wet edge? It dried, of course, creating visible overlaps. When you apply the wet roller over the dried cut-in band, the paint creates an overlap called "hat-banding." To correct this problem, you will have to apply two to four coats of paint, which will require more paint, time, and effort.

Hit the WALLS

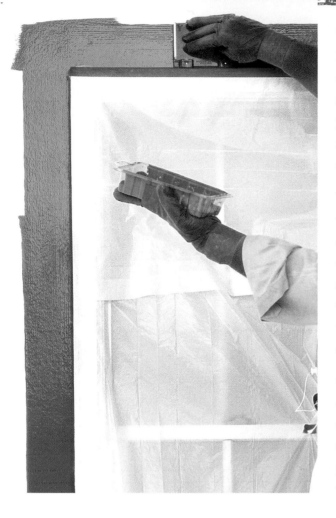

Clever cut-in

Be sure to mask all surfaces that you don't want to get paint on. Cut-in first, applying the paint swaths about 4 feet ahead of the roller person. Firmly grip the loaded tool with your dominant hand and apply the paint, keeping the tool in front of you. Have a platform ladder handy so you can easily reach all the surfaces.

Working in one direction, lay a 3- to 4-inch-wide band of wet paint along the inside edge of the wall. The wet band creates a dividing line of paint from one surface to the other—a "safety zone" so the roller person doesn't roll too close and get paint on the adjacent surfaces. Work from the bottom up, applying around the edges, first along the baseboards about 4 feet, then up and along the inside corners, and finally across at the ceiling line.

Cleaning small application tools, such as pads and brushes, about every two hours keeps dried paint from caking up on the tools, cleans out any particles of dirt that have accumulated over the course of your work, and helps prolong the life of these tools. After cleaning, spin them dry with a brush spinner before you start using them again.

quiz the WIZ
Should I paint the wall first or the trim?

Great question! If you are an amateur painter, do the trim work first, then the walls. This strategy will make it easier to sand, prepare, and paint all the details, edges, and planes of the trim work. After all the coats of paint on the trim work are thoroughly dry, mask off the trim work and paint the wall. Because you have masked the trim, any splatters from the wall will land on the masking tape, which will be removed later. Most professional painters would paint the wall first, then skillfully do the trim.

Room roll-out

The roll-out should be applied after the cut-in has been done and while the paint is still wet. Be sure to tape down drop cloths to protect the floor and give you safe footing. Attach an extension pole to the roller frame or use a telescoping handle. Load the roller cover with paint. Position the loading tray or bucket just ahead of your work section to keep you moving forward and reduce your body movements. Doing so also helps prevent roller dripping and bucket spills. Properly load the paint roller and start at the section to be painted. Keep the tool saturated with paint. If you must stop for a time, close up or wrap the tray and roller to keep them from drying.

Body position and mechanics are an important part of fast and effective painting. Stand with your feet spread about shoulder-width apart, always with your body facing the direction you're going to paint. This position, called the "A" stance, gives you better balance and leverage to reach bottom to top in one continuous stroke.

With the roller loaded, position yourself in front the section you want to paint. Place the roller on the surface and apply the paint to the wall. To avoid paint splatter, don't roll fast, but work at a comfortable rhythm and pace. After you have applied two or three roller widths on the wall, take a step to the side and repeat the same procedures. The cutter and the roller should be spaced no more than 4 to 6 feet apart; this spacing ensures the roller is always painting into the wet edge. Continue working around the room in this manner until it is completed.

tips 'n' tricks

Pull the masking tape off while the paint is fresh! Remove the masking materials within 45 to 60 minutes after the paint is applied to prevent surface tear-up. The idea of masking tape is to protect surfaces from the paint. However, if you slop the wet paint over the sealed masking tape, then let the paint cure to hard, the paint film will bond to both the wall and the masking tape. When you go to remove the tape, the film acts as one piece, tearing and ripping up the wall or trim work. To avoid this, pull the tape after the final coat of paint has started to set, but before it's completely dry. The result will be a clean edge with no tear-up.

Resurfacing PANELING

Yes, you can paint or apply wallpaper to paneling, but why? If you have real tongue-and-groove or beadboard paneling, it's worth keeping and refinishing. Otherwise, remove it or cover it with drywall. But if none of those solutions is practical, you can paint or apply wallpaper to it if you prepare the surface.

1. Make sure the paneling is secure to the wall studs. If you find any gaps or bowing, use wallboard screws or ring-shank paneling nails to level and stabilize the panels. Locate the studs behind the paneling, and drive the fasteners into the studs just beneath the surface of the paneling.

2. Scrub the surfaces with a sponge mop saturated in denatured alcohol, then wipe down with a clean cloth saturated in denatured alcohol to degrease and degloss the surface. Allow the paneling to dry overnight and apply a coat of white-pigmented oil-based sealer. Let it dry. Lightly sand the surface with 240-grit sandpaper, and wipe the surface with a tack cloth to remove the dust. Apply a second coat of sealer and let it dry.

3. Fill the grooves and any holes with exterior-grade surfacing compound. This material bonds and flexes better with the wood as it expands and contracts, preventing gaps and cracks that can emerge in time with regular wallboard joint compound. When the compound is dry, sand smooth and wipe clean. Apply a second coat of exterior grade compound; two or three light coats are better than one heavy coat. Finally, apply a third coat of sealer, let dry, and sand smooth.

4. Now you can safely install wallpaper, apply a faux finish, or paint the walls because you have stabilized, sealed, and smoothed the paneling.

Painting BRICKS and CONCRETE

Bricks, concrete, and other masonry surfaces call for some extra prep because of alkali and their coarsely textured, porous surfaces.

One problem is efflorescence—a white, powdery deposit that occurs when water migrates through concrete and mortar, then evaporates, leaving a mineral residue. Wait at least six months for new concrete or mortar to cure before painting. Before painting dry masonry or concrete, repair active leaks and remove the alkali deposits.

Seal the surface with a masonry sealer, then apply a coat of paint using a foam roller cover. Keep the sheen consistent and smooth by only rolling in one direction. Latex masonry paint works well on most interior masonry surfaces, including brick.

Painting concrete and brick floors

Make sure the surface is dry, moisture-free, and patched, if needed. Clean the floor with a TSP (trisodium phosphate) cleaner according to manufacturer's instructions.

If you plan to use oil-based paint, etch the concrete with a solution of 1 part muriatic acid (also known as hydrochloric acid) added to 10 parts water. For latex paint, use a phosphoric acid solution in the same ratio. Both acids are caustic chemicals, so exercise caution. Mix the solutions in a plastic pail, adding the acid to the water. Never pour water into acid; it can boil and splash out. Wear rubber gloves

and safety goggles while mixing and applying, and follow manufacturer's instructions.

When the floor is dry, vacuum up any dust, apply a sealer, then roll or brush on the finish coat.

For high-traffic areas and concrete exteriors such as garage floors, use epoxy paint. It dries harder, lasts longer, and is impervious to oil and stains. One caution: epoxy paints are slick. You might want to add special silicate, available from a home supply store, to create a nonslip surface. Many specialty masonry paints are available for surfaces such as floors and stairs. Ask a paint retailer to help you select the best kind of masonry paint for your surfaces and conditions.

tips 'n' tricks

Here are a few more tricks I've learned in my years as a Wall Wizard.

- *If bristles come off the brush, remove them from the painted surface with eyebrow tweezers or by touching them with the wet brush—they should cling to it. Wipe the brush with a clean cloth to remove stray bristles.*

- *Wipe paint off a paint shield after each use to keep the edge clean.*

- Disposable foam brushes don't work well for applying paint to large surfaces; they tend to drag it across the surface rather than let it flow. However, they do work well for very small touch-up jobs, and for varnishes, stains, and shellacs, creating glass-smooth finishes with few brush marks.

- When painting with enamel, work quickly and brush lightly. Overbrushing leaves streaks and marks. Do not touch up areas you've already painted. If you have problems, let the paint dry, degloss it, and repaint.

- Use a spray can or paint sprayer to paint heating system registers and grills.

● *For quick touch-ups, pour a small amount of paint into a clean shoe polish bottle; the pad is perfect for small jobs. Label the bottle with the room and color; snap on the lid to store.*

● You can make your own brush for small touch-ups. Simply clip a clothespin to a piece of sponge foam. Cut the point any shape you want to paint into corners or hard-to-reach places.

● Before you start painting, fill a couple of 1- or 3-gallon buckets with clean water. Have a synthetic tile sponge and plenty of towels handy throughout the job. Use them to quickly wipe up any spills. Change the water often so you don't put dirt back up on the surface. Dry the surface with a clean, dry towel to prevent water spots and stains.

● A concave roller does a great job on fixed shutters, radiator fins, and other rounded surfaces.

● *A beveled paint roller helps prevent paint buildup in corners.*

● *Paint pipes, wrought-iron balustrades, and other contoured surfaces with a paint mitt.*

chapter 5

Faux Finishing

ow that you've mastered the basics of painting, you're ready to move on to creating your own custom faux finishes. "Faux" is a French word that means "false," but faux finishes aren't so much false as illusory. They're painted finishes that can make a common plaster or wallboard wall look like something much more exotic—leather, marble, or fabric, for instance—along with a number of other effects that add depth, richness, and texture to a wall, creating a dramatic focal point in a room.

And I do mean dramatic. "That's so cool! How do you do that?" is an exclamation I hear all the time as I demonstrate faux finishes, such as rag-rolling, sponging, flogging, washing, and many more, in my workshops at home shows around the world. The question that inevitably follows my demonstration is "Can I do that?"

My answer: Sure! With the proper understanding of how to achieve each finish, almost anyone can create beautiful faux effects. And, as with basic painting, success is the result of two things: mastering the materials and knowing how to choose and use the tools of the trade. Once you know and master these basics, you can use your imagination to create a variety of results.

And as with painting, I don't expect you to create perfect results the first time—so why should you? I routinely practice my faux effects before letting loose on a wall. Faux finishing is an expressive art that transcends the technical, and some of the best techniques I've created have resulted from experimentation—and even from mistakes I've made that have revealed a different way to create the illusion. So go ahead and experiment! You never know what you might discover and create. And as with basic painting, if you don't like the result, just paint over it and start again!

In this chapter, you'll learn what glazes are and what they do. I've already told you that Wizards work wet, and in faux finishing, you'll take that directive to heart in a whole new way—to create a new dimension of finishes.

CONTRAST and Color

Faux finishing is all about creating a three-dimensional look on a two-dimensional surface. Walls have height and width, but they're flat surfaces and have no depth. A faux finish gives the wall the illusion of depth—the sense that you're not looking at the wall, but that you're looking into the surface.

At first, the idea of creating a three-dimensional look on a two-dimensional wall using nothing more than paint and glaze might sound a little strange. After all, faux finishes imitate natural materials that are flat, such as wood, stone, and leather.

Well, they're not actually flat. Leather, of course, has a surface texture. Stone, such as granite or marble, has a crystalline structure. Some of the minerals that make up the crystals are clear or translucent, so you actually look into the stone, sometimes only for microscopic distances, and sometimes, in the case of a largely translucent stone such as quartz, for quite a distance. Wood grain is similar. Some woods have grain that's so translucent it conducts light fiberoptically, causing the wood to shimmer and flash in direct light, giving it a gemlike quality.

Faux finishes recreate these natural surfaces in the same two ways. When we're applying a faux finish, we create *actual depth* by using a glaze—a semitransparent finish that allows us to see through the glaze layer and into the color of the paint underneath. The distance we see into the finish through the glaze is only the microscopic thickness of the glaze coat itself. But like the tiny quartz crystal embedded in a granite slab or the translucent wood fiber as thick as a human hair, that distance is enough to impart a sense of depth to the surface. I'll talk more about glazes later in the chapter.

As faux finishers, we control *apparent depth.* That's because apparent depth is the degree of contrast between a material's highlights and its shadows. Faux finishing always involves using at least two colors—a highlight color and a shadow color. The degree of contrast between these colors determines the apparent depth of the finish.

Often we use a darker-colored glaze over a lighter-colored base coat, but sometimes we reverse the situation and use a lighter-colored glaze over a darker-colored base coat. It all depends on the nature of the effect you want to create.

So there you have it: The magic of faux finishing is in fooling your eye with the illusion of highlights and shadows.

Instead of looking at two different colors of paint on a flat wall, the eye thinks it sees a rich, textured surface with depth.

There's even more! The colors you choose to combine and the tools and techniques you use to apply them determine what the resulting surface looks like. The art and craft of faux finishing can take a lifetime to explore. Even after 25 years, I'm still learning and creating new techniques, finding and using new tools (or often, common tools in uncommon ways), and experimenting, discovering new results.

But all faux finishes use the same principle—the contrast between highlight and shadow—to bring off their particular look. Keep this in mind as you read about and practice the techniques I share with you.

Is this faux real? I'm holding the genuine piece of marble, which I used as a guide to create the faux finish on the wall panel behind it.

While contrast plays an important role with faux effects, you also use the basic understanding of color that you learned about in chapter 1. By combining that understanding of color with what you'll be learning about contrast, you'll have the knowledge and understanding you need to begin faux finishing.

tips 'n' tricks

Faux effects are all about creating visual dimension where there is no physical dimension. Part of that effect is achieved by the nature of glaze itself. Unlike paint, glaze is semitransparent, allowing you to see through the top layer of the finish and glimpse the base coat underneath. But how much depth you perceive—something faux painters call the "depth of field" of a finish—depends on the degree of contrast between light and dark. In general, the higher the contrast between the base coat and glaze, the greater the perceived depth of field.

The Tree of KNOWLEDGE

A simple way to understand how painting relates to faux effects is to imagine a tree. Basic painting represents the trunk of a tree. Faux effects represent two branches of that tree: positive techniques and negative techniques, both of which I'll cover at length later in the chapter. The specialty effects are the tree's leaves: They're the decorative finishes that everyone sees, but in reality the trunk still holds the tree together. Underneath it all, the root system, or preparation, is what goes unseen but keeps the tree stable. You need to know the basics before you move on to the specialty effects.

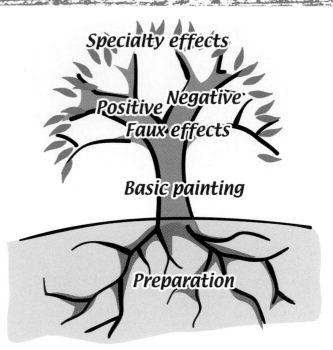

The three c's

Concept of faux effects refers to the color, style, furniture, and general design elements of a room that will guide you in choosing a faux effect. You must have a clear plan, or concept, to be successful in faux finishing.

Control is a question of mastering the medium. The control is the knowledge you have to produce an effect, as well as the tools that are used in this process. Hair clips, dish soap bottles, and sponge rollers are all examples of devices that help you control, or master, the medium of paint. Another aspect is how you control the ultimate painting tool—yourself. Be patient with yourself and your project partner, and understand that you will make mistakes

throughout the project. Your failure will ultimately bring success. This doesn't mean you can't experiment. In fact, some of my best finishes have resulted from mistakes. Make sure you feel comfortable and confident with the technique and tool before tackling an entire room. Remember, when you believe, you can achieve!

Character of the effect is the end result of your project. It's a combination of planning, procedures, the choices you make in your project partner and your faux finish tool, and your willingness to practice and make mistakes. You must be happy with your results; if not, practice until you are satisfied with the character of your project.

tips 'n' tricks

No FEAR—no **F**rustration, no **E**ffort, no **A**nxiety, and no **R**esistance to a project. Surprisingly, your greatest successes arise when you turn yourself over to the realm of possibilities. With no FEAR, a Wizard can move to the next step of taking RISKS. That means taking **R**esponsibility, **I**nterest, **S**elf-control, and **K**nowledge to understand the project, and taking away a feeling of **S**atisfaction from the project. When you take RISKS, you'll reap the rewards. The more you do, the better you get. Wizards aren't afraid to fail. They call it practice, and the more they do it, the better they get.

PREP Makes Perfect

Prep work is critical to any paint job. But it is far more important when faux finishing for several reasons:

● **You'll put several layers of finish on your walls,** rather than one or two simple coats. If your paint job fails due to poor preparation, you're out a lot more time and materials than if you had just done a basic, one-color job.

● **Depending on what type of faux finish you choose,** you may be flogging or whacking the wall with stiff-bristled brushes or other tools or pulling tools across its surface. This stresses the wall much more than a simple brush, roller, or spray application. A poorly prepared surface is less likely to withstand the rigors of such treatment.

● **Your faux painting may well end up being the focal point of your room**—one that gets a lot of attention. You don't want a poorly prepared surface to detract from the effect.

● **You'll use more materials and tools than with a basic paint job,** and you'll work faster. Once you get started it will be hard to stop to fix an imperfection because doing so will interrupt the job and ruin the effect.

● **Faux finishing is a messy job.** All those layers and all that whacking, dragging, flogging, and tapping means that paint will fly—even if you're the type who can paint a room without making a single drip or drop. You'll be glad you took the time to mask and protect surfaces properly.

● **To preserve the continuity of your decorative effect,** it's critical that you have the reach and range you need with each tool. Don't be caught short without the necessary ladder, scaffolding, or extension poles. While it can be inconvenient and risky during a traditional painting job, not having the right accessories can ruin a faux finishing job.

The first step in preparation is to gather the right tools for the job. You don't have to spend a lot of money to create successful faux finishes, but you do need the right equipment.

The key to handling materials is control. Liquids, for example, are always easier to deal with when wet than when dry. So choose tools that control paint and other liquids in their purest, wettest form. Paper dissolves when it comes into contact with water-based materials; metal rusts. Plastic is a great material; it keeps liquids in their wet state, doesn't interact with them, and forms a barrier to protect you and other surfaces.

cleaning tools

Use various sizes of plastic trash bags and resealable plastic bags to store hardware and switch plates. For dusty cleanup tasks, a shop vacuum cleaner, a push broom with dustpan, and dusting brush will come in handy. You'll need 5-gallon buckets, clean tile sponges for rinsing, a sponge-head floor mop with nylon scrubbing pads, and a nylon bristle deck brush with extension pole. Large household sponges with a nylon scrubbing pad, 2-quart plastic buckets, and lots of terry-cloth towels will round out your cleaning supplies.

SPECIALTY Tools

In addition to common painting tools such as paintbrushes, rollers, and plastic paint pans, decorative finishes require specialty tools to create certain effects. But that doesn't mean you have to go out and spend a hundred bucks for a special kit. In fact, some of the wackiest household tools create the most luxurious faux finishes. Remember to think off the wall and out of the can.

The Right Tool Rule states that things with handles, things made of plastic, and things that leave an impression are the most suitable for creating simple faux effects. A tool with **a handle** gives you a mechanical advantage, and it distances you from the surface you are working on. Why does this matter? You can see the effect emerge more clearly, and you keep yourself from being covered with glaze. **Plastic** is the easiest material to clean. **Things that leave an impression** offer an array of finishes that play upon highlight and shadow and create the optical illusion of depth in your faux effect.

It is also important to consider scale and perspective when choosing a tool to make an impression. The larger the tool, the larger the imprint. If used in a small room, a large tool can create a dramatic and sometimes overwhelming effect. When used in a larger room, the impression is proportional to the space.

cool tool

Size does matter! In conventional painting, tool size relates purely to applying paint in the most accurate, efficient manner. Faux painting, however, uses varying size tools for varying effects. Here, a broom-and-squeegee tool sold to spread and level driveway sealer is used to create a striated pattern. Cut notches in the rubber squeegee side and draw it down the wall to create a big, bold stripe pattern—in no time!

Tool ideas

When searching for a tool to create an effect, look for items made of plastic that have textural elements like bristles and fabric or a raised surface. Also look for items with a handle for ease of use. If you will be working on a large surface, look for large items. For example, a large, industrial dust mop will cover the surface in less time than a standard dust mop. A tip: Buy two of the same tool so that you will always have one to use and one that is drying while you work.

Here are some other tools to consider:

- Toilet cleaning brush
- Sea wool sponge
- Tongs
- Squeegee
- Fly swatter
- Bubble wrap
- Truck tire brush
- Terry cloth
- Duster car mop
- Barbecue brush

As I mentioned earlier, sometimes the wackiest items make the best effects. Where do I look for tools? In the automotive and household cleaning sections—you'll never look at Kmart or Walmart in the same way again!

quiz the WIZ

How far in advance can I paint the base coat?

Wait no more than a week to paint your faux finish on top of your base coat. Waiting longer will jeopardize the paint job because of everyday contaminants, such as hair spray, cooking oil, and general dust buildup. These contaminants put a film on the clean surface and prevent proper adhesion of the glaze.

What if I already have a satin finish on the wall?

You can apply glaze over an existing satin finish, but you first need to clean it with rubbing alcohol and scrub sponge (see chapter 3, "Preparation").

What lies beneath

Regardless of the effect you want to create, the first step in faux finishing is to paint a base coat on the wall. If you are a novice, begin with only two colors, then incorporate more complex combinations as you master a technique. Follow three rules when choosing a base coat:

- **Always paint the darker color on the wall.** OK, maybe not always, but if you're a novice, it is so much easier if the dark color is on the wall because it is easier to lighten a color than darken it. Use the lighter color in the top coat of glaze. This creates the illusion of a three-dimensional surface with highlights on top and shadows underneath.

- **Use satin or eggshell interior latex paint for your base coat.** Flat paint sucks—literally—because of its high porosity; it has no sheen value. On the other hand, satin latex paint has a slight sheen that is ideal for decorative effects.

- **Allow the base coat to dry completely before applying the top coat of glaze,** a minimum of 4 to 8 hours. If you don't, the chemicals in the top coat of glaze can dissolve the base coat of paint. I usually paint the base coat the day before I create the faux finish.

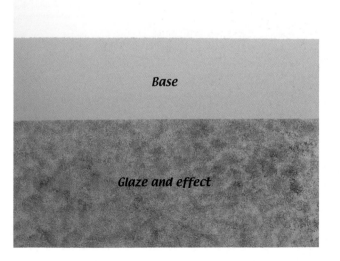

Sealer

Base

Glaze and effect

CONTROLLING Contrast

Applying a dark glaze over a light base coat results in a rich, dramatic look. Why? Because most home interiors are light colored, so adding dark creates a stark contrast. A dark element in most rooms draws the eye like a magnet.

Here's what it looks like when you roll a black glaze onto a white wall. Glaze isn't the same as paint—the pigments are diluted in a clear medium, resulting in a translucent finish. When glaze is rolled on evenly, it's all the same thickness, so the entire glazed surface has the same tone.

The magic of a faux finish lies in altering the thickness of the glaze, either by absorbing or displacing some of the wet glaze with a tool. The feather dusters I'm using here do both. Where the glaze is thinner, more of the white background shows through, creating a highlight. Where the glaze remains thick, less background shows through, creating a shadow. The contrast between highlight and shadow creates the appearance of depth, and the nature of the tool used creates the look of the specific effect. Because a dark-over-light effect usually has a dark tone, these effects are typically bold and dramatic.

Applying a light glaze over a dark base coat usually results in an effect with a soft, subtle look, because the tone of the effect is closer to the light tones typically present in home interiors. A light element in most rooms tends to float in the background, complementing but not distracting from architectural focal points, such as fireplaces or moldings, or from decorating focal points, such as furnishings or artwork.

Now look at the effect you get when rolling a white glaze over a black base coat. Note that the glaze doesn't appear pure white; its translucency allows some of the black base coat to show through. Manipulating the white glaze will allow even more of the base coat to show through, but the tone of the overall result will still be considerably lighter—and thus more subtle—than a dark-over-light effect.

You can use exactly the same tools and techniques with this effect as you can to create the dark-over-light effect—but notice how different the two results are! Although the glaze was manipulated in the same way, the light-over-dark effect has a much more subtle look. It's harder to discern the individual impressions of the tools, and the result has a soft, pleasingly out-of-focus appearance. Dark-over-light and light-over-dark techniques are equally effective—they just result in very different looks. If you keep in mind that almost any effect can be done either way, you've doubled your faux finishing repertoire!

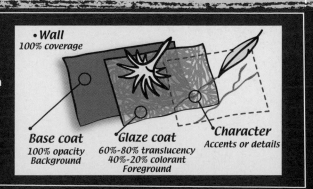

tips 'n' tricks

When you peel back the layers of a faux finish, you can see how they work together to create the illusion of three dimensions. The tools manipulate the paint coats; the combination of background, foreground, and accents fools your eyes into seeing depth.

• **Wall**
100% coverage

Base coat
100% opacity
Background

Glaze coat
60%-80% translucency
40%-20% colorant
Foreground

Character
Accents or details

My Mistake

LESS IS MORE

On one job, I had completed a sample board of a faux marble effect and shared it with the customer. He really liked it, and we both signed off on it.

I was training an apprentice at the time, and I thought this job would be a good chance to give him some experience in faux marble technique.

I gave him my half of the sample board, which replicated the entire technique. I went over the steps used to create this technique in great detail, making sure he understood what must be done at each step. He was already quite skilled in other faux effects, and he listened attentively and watched my demonstration of how to get started carefully. Eventually, I left him to his work, confident that he'd do a good job.

When I returned at the end of the day, I was stunned—no, disoriented—by what I saw on the wall. It was technically flawless—the detail work and veining were first-class. But something was terribly wrong. The design had none of the subtlety and lightness I'd originally envisioned. It looked too crowded, busy, and contrasty—not at all like the delicately veined, milky-white marble I'd replicated on my sample board.

I took out the board and held it up to the wall. I immediately saw what had happened. My apprentice made an exact replica of about a quarter of my design—the most contrasty portion. The rest of the field he'd completely ignored!

After a quick conversation, I soon found out what had happened. The subtle parts of the design were too delicate for his eye to see and his still-evolving technique to replicate. So he concentrated on the high-contrast, easier-to-execute portion of the design. It was as though, given a big, beautiful landscape of a misty field with a single tree standing in it, he reproduced the tree—only over and over and over, with no background to give it context and scale.

Lesson learned: Drama, contrast, and detail are great—in context. The eye needs some relief. Details need a field to frame them. You have to step back from the wall every so often as you work and look at the effect as a whole. Go easy on detail, especially when you're starting out. Let your focal points have plenty of space around them. Don't crowd the wall with detail. Less IS more. And if, after stepping back, you decide to add more veining, stronger color, a bit more detail, you easily and quickly can. But if your design is too dense, claustrophobic, and busy, you have no choice but to paint over all your hard work and start again.

That GLAZED Look

Glaze modifies the color of a base coat of paint by allowing it to peek through a translucent filter. Think of glaze as the lens in sunglasses. You can see through a tinted lens, but the view is altered. Use a glaze when you want to create visual depth of highlight and shadow.

Here's the main reason some people buy this book—for the recipe of my amazing Wall Wizard Glaze! If you mix as directed, you'll have the perfect potion for faux finishing.

Wall Wizard Glaze

½ **quart satin or eggshell latex interior paint.** Remember to use the lighter color of your two-color combination.

2 quarts glazing medium. This glazing medium is actually paint without color. It pulls the paint color molecules apart to create the translucent or semitranslucent effect of glaze.

½ **quart water.** Water is the thinning medium that makes it easier to work with the glaze.

6 ounces Floetrol. A binding medium, Floetrol is a Wall Wizard wonder. It stops blistering, cracking, mold, and mildew. It makes the color last three to four years longer, and it conditions the paint, making it sticky and gooey so the glaze sticks to the wall without running. Floetrol can be found at home supply stores.

4 drops fabric softener or ¼ teaspoon per gallon of paint. This household product acts as an extending agent, preventing the glaze from drying too quickly.

Combine all ingredients in a clean, 1-gallon juice jug, and shake for about three minutes before using to keep the mixture from separating. In fact, every time you pick up your container of glaze, give it a shake before using—just make sure the lid is sealed tightly.

A 1-gallon juice jug makes the perfect container because it is made of plastic, so it won't corrode. It has a handle and an airtight seal, both of which are ideal for storing paint. And it holds enough glaze for 1,500 square feet, which will cover approximately two 10×15-foot rooms.

To make more or less glaze, use one part paint color to four parts glazing medium. The remaining ingredients are proportionate to this recipe.

How much glaze do you need? More than enough to cover your project! Seriously, you will never ever be able to match a paint color, so if you run out of glaze before you finish, you might as well start over. Always make twice as much glaze as you think you will need.

tips 'n' tricks

Instead of lugging around a gallon of glaze, fill a 1-quart dish soap bottle. The bottle has an airtight seal, it's easy to control, you can squeeze out just the amount you need, and, most importantly, if you drop it, you won't get glaze all over everything!

POSITIVE Thinking

Faux finishes can be divided into either positive or negative techniques. Loading a tool with glaze and applying it to the wall is a positive technique—you are adding glaze to the wall. Covering the wall with a coat of glaze and then using a tool to remove it is a negative technique because you are taking glaze away from the wall. No matter what faux finish you want to achieve, you will use either a positive or negative technique.

Positive techniques in decorative finishing are the hardest to achieve because you have to get the effect even. It requires *tactile response,* the feedback you receive from the pressure you put on the tool. More pressure on the tool creates less detail because the tool, a sponge for example, is compressed against the wall. Less pressure creates more detail, because the points of the sponge surface make contact.

It usually takes three tries to get the hang of a technique: Your first try will be a failure; your second will be better; and by the third, you'll start to see the effect you want. Here's the basic technique:

1. Lay out two plastic plates and squeeze glaze onto one. Use masking tape to attach the other to your "off" hand.

2. Load the tool by dipping it into the glaze three times: "Dippy, dippy, dippy."

3. Unload or lighten the load of glaze on the tool by tapping it on a clean plate three times: "Tappy, tappy, tappy." This also serves to distribute the glaze evenly on the tool.

4. Gently touch the wall with the tool, keeping your hand parallel to the wall as you work. The tool should move perpendicular to the surface.

5. Rotate your wrist one-quarter turn as if you were turning a doorknob. Your process repeats over and over: Tap, pick up the tool, rotate, tap, pick up the tool, rotate, and so on, turning your hand to a different position each time. Reload the tool.

Work in a spiral motion in 4-foot sections instead of straight across to avoid making a pattern. Work from the bottom up and into your field of view. A positive finish looks best when it is randomly applied on the surface. Avoid creating rows, columns, or any sort of structure in the finish.

tips 'n' tricks

- Start on a practice wall to master your technique. Laundry rooms and guest rooms are a good choice—not the living room or kitchen where your mistakes will be visible. Be sure to prep the wall.

- Always dampen your tool in a solution of fabric softener and water to prevent the glaze from sticking to the tool. The solution also softens the tool to make the paint application easier. To make sure the tool is not too wet, cover the tool with a towel and wring out the excess solution.

- Make sure the molding is covered with tape or plastic so you can get into corners with your faux finish tool.

- Have two tools on hand: one to use and one that is drying while you work. When one tool is saturated with paint, clean it in a solution of fabric softener and water, then use the other tool while the first one dries.

4

5

cool tool

Clamp a hair clip to a sponge to create the perfect handle. Hair clips are made of plastic so they're easy to clean, they make the sponge ergonomic so it's easier to hold, and they make it simple to control the sponge during application. Clips make it a cinch to sponge in corners and hard-to-reach areas.

NEGATIVE Finishes

Negative techniques require two roles to create a successful faux finish: the glazer and the whacker. The glazer applies glaze to the wall from the floor up. The whacker "whacks" the wall from floor to ceiling with the tool to create the effect by removing glaze. You can do negative finishes solo, but the technique really works much better when you team up with another person.

Working as a pair makes the job go more quickly; you get better results when working in assembly-line fashion. The glazer cuts-in and rolls on the glaze; the whacker works 4 to 6 feet behind the glazer. Don't let one get too far ahead or behind; the glaze will dry and you will get out of rhythm. If you must work alone, work in 4-foot-wide sections, floor to ceiling, so the glaze doesn't dry while you are applying the faux effect.

One of the great things about negative finishes is that if you make a mistake—while the glaze is still wet—you can simply "erase" it by reglazing over the area and whacking it again.

Above all, make sure you practice, practice, practice your techniques. The moment of truth comes when you apply the glaze to the wall for the first time. If you're already accustomed to working with the glaze, your results will be dramatically better.

wizard WARNING

Whatever you do, don't change whackers in the middle of a project! Doing so will completely change "the hand" (the effect), because different people apply different pressure and rotate their wrists differently while whacking a wall. The result will be two different finishes with an awkward break where they change—probably not the effect you're going for.

tips 'n' tricks

Rhythm is an important part of faux finishing. Getting in the groove—that is, pacing and timing your application as you paint—will help you control and create consistency throughout your effect. It's all about keeping the glaze wet from one section to the next as you work vertically and horizontally across the wall with your tool. A tip: Play music while you work. It makes it easier to establish rhythm in your technique.

Also make sure that you work in the direction in which you feel most comfortable. If two people are working on a project, then you both need to work in the same direction; it will be easier to keep your rhythm, balance, and coordination. And try to work directly in front of yourself—your field of vision and your control of the tool will be much better.

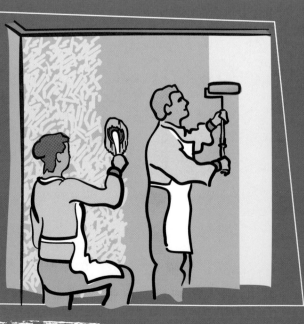

My Mistake

Our culture doesn't have a large vocabulary for color or visual effects, so it's easy to get off on the wrong foot when you use words alone to describe the effect you want—whether you're talking to your painting contractor or to your spouse.

"Just do a rag finish in this room," the client told me, so after agreeing on the color, I did. She hated it, so I painted over it and did it differently. She hated that too.

It didn't take a genius to see we were having a communication problem. Since I'd just worked for two days for nothing, I decided to spend a little time trying to figure out a way to communicate exactly what I was going to do without having to paint the whole room first. I don't mind rejection—I just don't like it to take all day!

The problem is that a single descriptive word, such as "ragging," can describe a tremendous variety of finishes. There had to be a better way.

That day, I bought a stack of canvas-covered boards from my local craft store. Now, after discussing a finish with a client, I come back to my studio and execute it on the board. Then I bring the board to our next meeting. If the client likes the finish, I cut the board in half then and there. We both sign each half of the board. The customer keeps one half, I keep the other. If the finish on the wall matches the finish on the board, the customer is obliged to pay for the job. If not, I do it over for free (something, I'll add, that I've never had to do).

That helped a lot, but not enough. People were still surprised by what they ended up with—even though they could see that the finish we executed exactly duplicated the sample on the board. Now, I go one step further, encouraging clients to tack the board up on the wall that they want finished, and look at it several times a day in different light. If they find the effect too dark, too light, too subtle, or too dramatic, we can adjust the shade or tint of the color, and the contrast between highlight and shadow to fine-tune the finish to their sensibility, and to the wall's location and lighting.

Still, it can be hard for someone unaccustomed to faux finishing to visualize the finished effect as it looks on an entire wall. I still have to resort to the sample boards every once in a while to show someone I did create exactly the finish they'd specified.

Lesson learned: Don't assume you can visualize the look of a finish from a simple description—or even from a small sample. Practice on a large span of wall in your basement or garage first, so you know what the effect looks like when writ large on a wall—before you attack your living room.

How ABSORBING!

Sponging is what most people think of when they think of a faux finish, and for good reason: It's a versatile and attractive effect.

Sponging is the iconic faux finish technique—the softly stippled, almost impressionistic look it creates is among the most recognizable and widely used of all the faux finishes. It creates a soft background that is a great foil for solid, geometric elements within a room. Spaces with lots of molding or strong architectural elements such as dormers, windows, doors, and built-ins and rooms that feature bold furnishings or artwork often benefit from sponge-finished walls. Such walls can be ideal hosts: They increase a room's sense of space. Given the right choice of base color and glaze, they can also harmonize a room's many different elements.

It is also, ironically, the most difficult basic effect to do. That's because it is the technique, not the tool, that creates the look. Practice—on a scrap piece of wallboard or the closet in a back bedroom—is essential before you tackle your living room wall.

Expect to experiment for awhile before you get the hang of this technique. The idea is to create as random a look as possible, and to avoid a columns-and-rows effect by rotating your wrist before you bring the sponge in contact with the wall. That's because unlike manufactured artifacts, natural materials often have a random appearance.

sea sponges

A natural sea sponge is one of the oldest faux finishing tools—and one of the best. Unlike synthetic sponges, each one is unique, imparting a random, highly textured look to your project. They absorb and manipulate glaze well, and they're reusable and incredibly durable: Wash and rinse them out and they return to their original shape, ready for the next job.

Get at least one good-sized sea sponge. The larger the sponge, the more textural choices you have, as each face of the sponge will offer you different options. Also, the bigger the sponge, the faster your job will go, and the less fatiguing your project will be. While you're at it, pick up a hair clip from a beauty or discount store. The clip's spring-loaded teeth will help you hold onto the sponge, especially when the tool is saturated with slippery glaze. A set of long-handle tongs is a good accessory as well, allowing you to easily reach into corners and the tops of tall walls.

Sponge positive

The sponge positive technique adds a glaze of a contrasting color to a base coat. Here the base coat is light, and the glaze is a couple shades darker. As with all faux techniques, you apply the base coat first and allow it to dry overnight. Then take the following steps:

1. **Start applying the glaze.** If you're right-handed, work from right to left and from the bottom of the wall up. This method allows you to work at arm's length, reducing fatigue and providing enough distance to see how the effect develops. Since you are more likely to make a mistake early in the job, before you get used to the tool, starting at the bottom keeps any faux pas well below eye level.

2. **Open and close the door.** Tap the wall with the sponge, lift the sponge off the wall surface, then rotate your wrist before tapping the wall again. I call the wrist rotation "opening and closing the door" as it imitates the motion you make when twisting a doorknob. Doing so increases the randomness of the effect, because the sponge hits the wall in a different orientation with each tap. Make sure the sponge is not in contact with the wall when you rotate your wrist, however, or you'll get little tornado-shaped, blurred twist marks on the wall that will disrupt the look.

3. **Don't create columns and rows.** We're not striving to be accountants here. To avoid creating a linear pattern like this one, work in about a 30-foot square area of the wall at a time, creating an imaginary box, then spiraling in from the edge. When you're done, blend the section into the one next to it.

4. **Stop, wash, and rinse out your sponge—** or switch to your second sponge—when the tool becomes saturated with glaze to the point that the effect is about to change. How do you know? Practice!

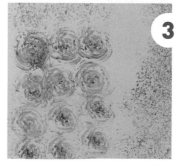

1

2

Sponge negative

The sponge negative effect uses the sponge to manipulate glaze and remove it from the wall—not to apply it, as with sponge positive. To create this technique, have a partner apply the glaze to about 4 feet of wall area while you follow and "sponge off." You really need two people, as you want to sponge off the glaze shortly after it is applied. If too much time passes, the glaze will begin to dry, and the effect won't be homogeneous. For that reason, it's best to practice this technique in a room with approximately the same temperature and humidity as the room you plan to finish so you learn just how much working time you have before the glaze starts to set. The sponge negative technique is actually easier to do well than sponge positive, and is more forgiving of mistakes: If you really mess up, you can just reglaze and start again.

1. **Same technique.** Use the same approach as with sponge positive—work from the bottom up, starting with the side of the room that corresponds with your dominant hand. Remember to work in a box, spiral in and blend the effect, rotate your wrist, and change sponges before the effect degrades.

2. **Different results.** The look of sponge negative, however, is strikingly different from sponge positive. Sponge negative leaves more of the glaze on the wall, resulting in a softer, more mottled, less pixilated look.

tips 'n' tricks

Here are a few faux finishing terms that will help you understand and communicate faux techniques:

Positive effect: A faux finish created by applying glaze to a surface with a tool.

Negative effect: A faux finish created by removing glaze from a surface with a tool, or by manipulating the glaze while it is still wet.

Reverse: An effect featuring a darker glaze over a lighter background.

Tactile response: The "feedback" a faux finishing tool communicates to its user during the finishing process. With experience, you'll learn by tactile response the amount of hand pressure on the tool that's needed to create the effect. Start out with a light touch, as it's easier to hit the wall again, and harder, but you can't "take back" a hit that's too forceful.

Aspect orientation: The rotational position of the tool as it hits the wall. By rotating your wrist, you change a sponge's aspect orientation, increasing the randomness of the effect.

From RAGS to Richness

Rag-rolling imparts a rich, textured finish fast—and is one of the easiest faux finishes to master. It is a bit of a fantasy abstraction—you're not trying to recreate a certain material, so you can be a bit random and carefree in your application. You're trying to create artful chaos.

Rag-rolling is one of the easier faux finishing effects to create, and one of the fastest to apply. The reason for both of these attributes is this: Unlike sponge painting, which is all about technique, rag-rolling is an effect where you can let the tool do the work and simply enjoy the process.

And the results are great. I describe the finish as a "pseudo leather" look, because the completed effect suggests the softness, the folds, wrinkles, and grain of leather, without specifically trying to reproduce the look, feature for feature, of a real piece of cowhide.

The first rag-rolled effects were created by literally twisting and rolling a piece of fabric into something that looked like a big wrinkled sausage, then rolling it over the wall with bare hands. As you might imagine, this process took forever and was very messy. Some purists still finish walls this way, but when technology can help you do a better job faster, I'm all for it. Like most professional faux finishers, I create this effect by wrapping a twisted rag around a paint roller or by using a special roller of my own design (see the "tips 'n' tricks" sidebar at the bottom of this page).

Once the tool is ready to go, it's just a matter of making several passes over the wall at different angles to create the random effect. The more passes you make, and the more angles you employ, the more subtle and natural your effect will look—so go nuts!

Rag 'n' roll

To complete the ragging effect, you need a rag, a roller, and some rubber bands to attach the rag to the roller. I recommend using a foam roller, because it will even out the pressure on the rag, keeping it in contact with the wall surface at all times. This results in a more even application (or removal) of glaze, and a softer, more abstract, more pleasing effect than a conventional fuzzy roller, which has less "give." You can wrap the roller with all kinds of materials. I describe some of my favorites and the effects they create on page 141.

tips 'n' tricks

To make rag-rolling even easier, I use a commercially made roller with a rag that's permanently stitched on. The result is a more evenly mottled effect, and easier application. You don't need to roll and rubber-band the rag on, or deal with removing it once it's saturated with glaze.

Rag negative

As with other faux effects, ragging can be positive or negative: Positive adds glaze with the rag roller to a base coat that's applied previously and allowed to dry overnight; negative partially removes glaze from a wall while the glaze is still wet. I prefer the negative effect as it adds a natural, organic quality to a room.

1. **Glaze the wall.** Glaze about a 4-foot section at a time to ensure that the glaze is still wet when you rag-roll it. Because the rag roller allows you to work fast, you don't need a partner to create this effect, although it goes more smoothly if you do.

2. **Rag off.** Start by drawing the rag roller diagonally across the wall, maintaining even pressure and speed. Practice will tell you what works best. Press too hard or roll too fast and the effect degrades—and glaze starts to fly! Even at moderate rolling speeds, you'll want to have other surfaces well masked and covered, since the uneven surface of the rag roller flings the glaze around a bit.

3. **Make repeated passes at different angles.** Make your second pass at right angles to the first. Notice how the effect becomes much softer and random where the two roller trails overlap. That's what you're after, and the more passes you make at different angles, the more subtle and layered the effect. So roll on, changing angles constantly.

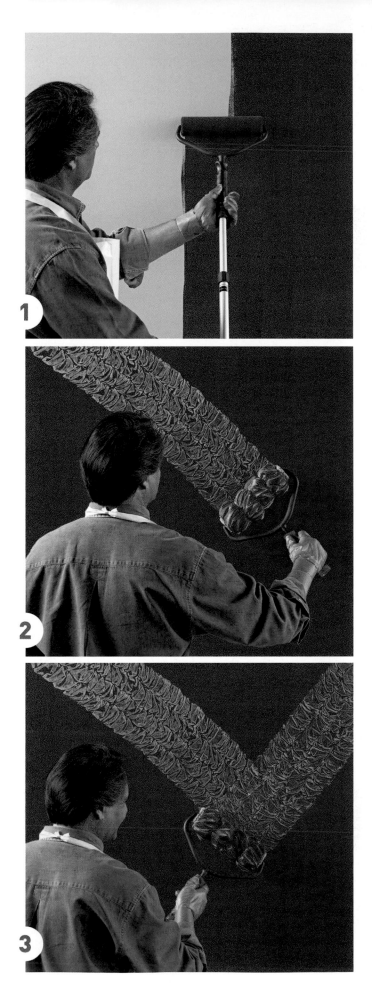

cool tools

Rag-rolling can produce a tremendous variety of effects because just about anything you can wrap around a paint roller—burlap, lace, plastic, bubble wrap, chamois, terry cloth, old T-shirts, you name it—can be used to absorb or make an impression in the wet glaze. And each material creates a different look. Here are a few of my favorites.

BUBBLE WRAP   Ragging allows you to really step out of the box when it comes to tools. Bubble wrap is great stuff—it's got a coarse texture already, so you don't need to twist it when applying it to the roller, which makes prepping the tool easier. Because it's plastic, it won't absorb glaze, but it will displace it. The effect is a bit softer than with an absorbent material, and also allows the roller to be used longer between cleanings, since the glaze doesn't load up nearly as quickly as it will on fabric. And, when it does come time to clean it, the glaze comes off right away.

TERRY CLOTH   Terry is the opposite of bubble wrap: highly absorbent, yet very finely textured. For that reason, I generally give terry a twist when applying it to the roller, and secure it with rubber bands. Unlike bubble wrap, which produces an even effect over the full width of the roller, the terry-covered roller will leave two stripes where the rubber bands depress the cloth and clamp it to the roller. You need to make more paths over the surface than with bubble wrap in order to roll out those stripes and create a random, unpatterned surface. The swirling veins left on the surface by twisted terry are a classic ragged look, perhaps most closely approximating leather.

PLASTIC SHEETING   Like bubble wrap, plastic sheeting lets you combine a high-tech material with a time-honored technique, expanding your creative options. I like to crinkle and twist the plastic as I apply it to the roller, overlapping several layers of the thin material for more texture. Like bubble wrap, it can be used quite a while before you need to clean the roller, and it, too, displaces rather than absorbs glaze. The result, though, looks surprisingly natural: like the crystal structure in quartz.

Bubble wrap

Terry cloth

Plastic sheeting

STRIATION Creation

Combing and dragging are a pair of techniques that are simpler than they look, and they produce great results.

Combing and dragging can be bold or subtle, large scale or small scale, dramatic and contemporary or soft and old-world. No matter what result you're after, you use the same relatively simple technique. What makes the difference are the choice of the tool you use, the color choices you make and, believe it or not, the amount of pressure you apply when you drag the tool down the wall. (Greater pressure, ironically, yields a softer effect.) **Combing** is a technique for displacing glaze with a comblike tool, such as a rubber squeegee with notches cut in its blade. It produces crisp, bold stripes. **Dragging** displaces glaze, but it also pulls and blends it at the same time. It produces a softer, less-contrasty effect.

As with many faux techniques, combing and dragging originated in France, where they were invented to emulate the beautiful striped fabrics used as wallpaper in the homes of the wealthy and called *strié* or stripes. Because the results can be so varied and you can work so fast, I've applied combed finishes to ceilings, floors, and furniture as well as walls in just about every type of room you can imagine. So go nuts! All you're risking is your time and a can of paint. Although the surface looks richly textured, that's all it is—a look. The actual surface is still flat, so you can sand, prime, and repaint a combed finish just as easily as a monochromatic wall.

cool tools

Combing and dragging are tool-driven techniques and invite technological experimentation. Traditionally, faux finishers dragged a comb, paintbrush, or broom through glaze to produce the effect. We still use those tools today, but now there are several additional options.

Wallpaper smoothing brushes are great because they have a narrow row of coarse nylon bristles that leave a distinctive texture—plus the brush is 12 inches wide, speeding your work. **Rubber window squeegees** also make terrific dragging tools, as their blades displace glaze well and can easily be notched to create a variety of scales and patterns. You can even attach long handles to squeegees when working in tall rooms and stairwells. For really dramatic looks in large spaces, I like to use a **driveway surfacing broom** and a **squeegee** with large-scale notches cut in the blade.

Combing and dragging effects

Unlike other faux techniques, combing and dragging involves simple, one-directional, repetitive motions. So if you're not comfortable with the random, abstract nature of, say, sponging, combing might be a great place for you to start. Paint your base coat and let it dry overnight (you can also use white as a base coat, as I have here). Mix up your glaze, which is typically the same hue as the base coat, but a bit lighter or darker (I used a much more dramatic contrast here so the effect would be easy for you to see). As with other faux finishes, you want an eggshell or satin finish for the base. Unlike flat paint, satin finish helps the glaze adhere to the wall without absorbing it, making your job easier.

1. **Roll on the glaze** using the three-stroke, up-down-up method. Overlap your strokes slightly to maintain a wet edge. To avoid the glaze drying too quickly, limit your work to a 4×8-foot section of wall at a time. If you find your glaze is a bit too dry to work easily by the time you've finished a section, either glaze smaller sections at a time or add just a bit of Floetrol or fabric softener to the glaze to extend working time.

2. **It's a drag!** Take your tool—here I'm using a conventional paintbrush—and drag it straight down the wall from top to bottom. Feel free to experiment with the dragging pressure and angle—notice I'm dragging the length of the bristles down the wall here, not just the tips, for a coarser effect. More pressure also yields more contrast.

3. **Use different tools for different effects.** Wallpaper smoothing brushes are terrific: Their narrow row of coarse bristles gives a wall character, and they rinse out quickly and easily. Plus their size allows you to do a foot-wide swipe at a time, reducing the time on larger jobs.

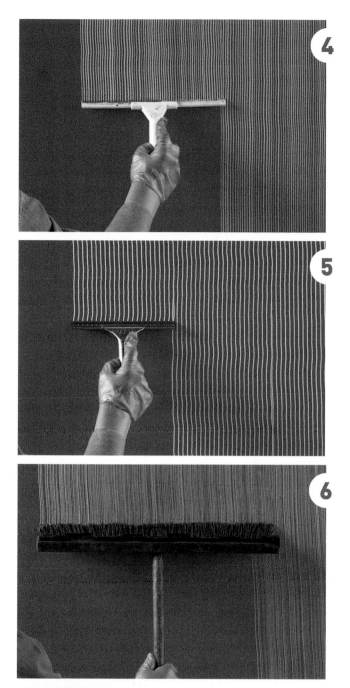

4. Window squeegees are one of my favorite combing tools. The rubber blades displace nearly all the glaze they come in contact with, resulting in sharp, high-contrast lines. Notch little "v" cutouts in the blades with a utility knife or nail clippers to create a comblike edge. Nibble away at it randomly with nail clippers for an abstract pattern like this, or . . .

5. Keep to the straight and narrow by carefully measuring and marking the rubber edge, then cutting precise, evenly spaced notches in it to create a highly regular striped effect.

6. A trip to the home center store will reveal even more tool options. This squeegee and broom combination is sold to spread and level driveway sealer, but its coarse texture and big scale make it a great combing tool. I'm using the bristles here, but notching the squeegee side of the tool offers another clever option. Tools such as these that have handles have better ergonomics. Rotate your wrist up when you reach the bottom of your stroke so you can drag all the way to the floor.

3 ways to finish

● The simplest form of combing involves making a single, top-to-bottom vertical pass down the glazed wall with your tool. This is the fastest way to execute the technique and yields crisp results.

● Multiple passes through the glaze are a second option. The effect tends to soften with each succeeding pass as the tool marks blend and layer. The result is a bit more subtle and lower in contrast. So if you think one pass looks a bit coarse or stark, take a few more swipes at the wall.

● Combing again after the glaze partially dries produces a third effect. The glaze moves differently in its partially dried, gel-like state. It can be fun to experiment with recombing the glaze at varying degrees of "set" to find what produces the effect you like best.

HIT the Wall

Flogging is pretty basic: you pick up a brush or mop and give the wall a good whack. It's fun, and results vary widely with tool choice.

Flogging is what I call a "portal technique." Once you understand flogging, you understand faux finishing.

I like people to start with this simple technique: Pick up a common household tool like a duster, a mop, or even a lowly toilet cleaning brush and whack it against a wall. If you can do that, you can create a faux finish.

Of course, there's a bit more to it than that, but much faux finishing is about unlearning what we've been taught about painting since kindergarten: Stay within the lines, and don't make a mess.

I say cut loose and have fun! Go ahead—WHACK that wall and see what happens. Whack it every which way—the more randomly the better. And don't worry about precision and detail—at least not with this effect. Flogging is not about detail. It's about creating an overall impression. I actually encourage people to work faster than they think they can, to pick up two tools, one in each hand and have at it. Once you free yourself from the tyranny of your left brain—the logical, tidy, think-inside-the-box side of your head—amazing things can happen. And the things you learn flogging are directly applicable to other faux techniques.

There are other reasons I love this technique: It's fast. It can produce incredibly varied results. And it's a good workout!

cool tools

I divide flogging tools into two categories: flogging tools and whacking tools. Both have long handles for leverage, and for reaching the tops of high walls and into corners.

Flogging tools are absorbent. They can either apply or suck up glaze, and include mops, dusters, and other tools that create a random pattern when they hit the wall—a pattern that changes with each strike.

Whacking tools, on the other hand, are not absorbent; instead, they displace glaze. These include various types of plastic brushes. I've found that truck tire brushes and toilet cleaning brushes work great, since they're tough, easy to clean, and wonderfully ergonomic.

You use both flogging and whacking tools with the same striking motion, but they make a different sound when hitting the wall—hence the different names.

Think negative

You CAN apply glaze to a wall by flogging or whacking—called a positive effect—but I don't recommend starting with that technique. Taking glaze off—called a negative effect—is easier to do, since you can always take off a bit more, refining the results as you go. If you really screw up, simply reroll the glaze and start again. On the other hand, if you're working on a positive effect and hit a wall too hard, use an overloaded tool, or go over an area too often with a glaze-loaded tool, there's not much you can do to fix your mistake. So to begin with, anyway, think negative!

1. **Apply the glaze.** Just roll it on over a satin or eggshell base coat that has cured overnight. When you're working, keep your tool right in front of your body where you can see it and control it most easily, not off to one side where you have to lean, twist, and strain to use it. I am working off to the side in many of these photos, but only so you can look over my shoulder and see what I'm doing. I usually work with my arms straight in front of me and move across the wall with my whole body as the effect progresses.

2. **Start whacking.** After glazing about a 4×8-foot wall section, pick up a tool or two and start striking the wall. The tools should be clean and moist—wring them out or pat them dry with a terry towel so they are able to absorb the glaze. Using two tools at once allows you to go twice as fast. Here I'm using a couple of tire brushes, but often I'll use different tools in each hand—one with a fine texture, for example, and one with a coarse one—to add depth and variety to the finish.

3. **Varied tools create varied results.** These small car mops create a randomly mottled effect, which can vary with the thickness of the glaze and the force of the impact with the wall. Generally you want to hit the surface hard enough to create an impression, but not so hard that you wear yourself out after a few blows, or damage the base coat or wall.

4. Keep the surface of the tool parallel with the wall, but constantly vary the angle it hits the wall. If this photo were a video, you'd see me almost dancing away with my upper body as I flogged, rotating my shoulders, my elbows, and my wrists to make sure the tool didn't hit the wall at the same angle twice. Failing to vary the angle produces a patterned series of impressions—not the random, mottled look you're after.

5. Brushes create a stippled look. The soft, impressionistic result varies with the size of the brush, the arrangement of the bristles, and how many passes you make over a given area.

6. Mops create a mottled look. The soft, random pattern of a dust mop is coarser, but also more muted and less grainy than a brush's stippling. Here, I'm using a large car duster—handy for doing large areas quickly, and creating a larger-scale texture than the smaller mop shown in photo 3.

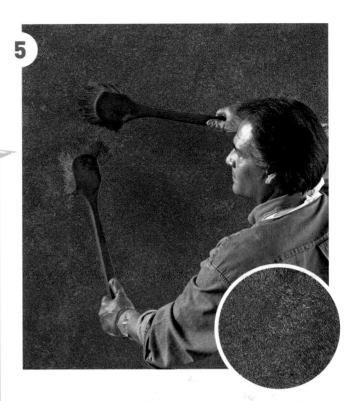

go ahead: paint yourself into a corner!

One of the things I like about flogging tools—especially car mops and tools with similarly floppy heads—is that they work in corners too. With other effects such as sponging, you often have to resort to smaller-scaled tools to reach into corners, but the mop's individual strands of yarn extend outward from the plastic head, reaching right into corners and up to moldings. That means you don't have to change tools as you approach an edge or corner. And that saves you time and makes it easy to preserve the continuity of the effect.

A tip: Get a feel for how far out from the plastic tool head the yarn extends, so you don't hit the adjacent wall with the solid head of the mop, creating a blur. Remember to mask anything you don't want pigment on, of course.

All WASHED Up

Washes take a bit of practice to execute—but the soft, subtle, aged effects they create make them a rewarding choice.

Washing is all about tonal values—creating varying intensities of the same hue. The glazes are applied with a sponge, then partially "washed off" with another sponge, leaving a very soft, ethereal, antiqued look that some people describe as "Tuscan" or "weathered." Unlike some other faux effects, it isn't designed to replicate a particular material. Perhaps for that reason, a wash is a great backdrop: It is better at showcasing furnishings and artwork than more representational effects. Yet it still adds drama and depth, because like other faux effects, it is composed of highlights and shadows.

Washes also suggest antiquity, for several reasons. First, a washed surface looks weathered, as though bleached by the sun and eroded by the wind and rain over the course of time. The finish also replicates the look produced by early, primitive paints, such as whitewash or milk paint, which were fine-grained pigments suspended in water or milk, and resulted in an uneven and somewhat translucent effect as their pigments gradually wore away.

Although they look subtle and primitive, washes are not particularly easy to achieve. First, you're starting with a positive effect, sponging glaze on the wall. Then, you switch to a negative process—sponging glaze back off again, but with a different sponge. Your ultimate aim is to create slight variations in tonal values, and effectively doing so takes practice.

cool tools

Washing is a hand effect and, unlike rag-rolling, there's no technological shortcut to make the job any faster, easier, or better. Since you're literally "washing" pigment onto or off of the wall, a good sponge is your primary tool. I usually use a **natural sea sponge** (with a hair-clip handle—see page 131) for the initial application, and a **synthetic tile sponge** for blotting and further refining the finish. You'll also need an **application tray.**

I use a TV tray—the cheap, stamped-steel kind with metal legs and a nice deep, lipped edge—as a mobile worktable on which to set my sponges and application tray. I cover the tray with several layers of extra-large aluminum foil. When I'm done, I just peel off the aluminum foil, exposing the next layer—no cleaning!

That glazed look

One of the secrets to a good wash finish is how thick to mix the glaze. Use the glaze formula on page 129, but thin it with a bit more water. Exactly how much more is a matter of judgment, like how much flour to add when making gravy. The precise mixture depends on temperature, humidity, surface porosity, and glaze color. Start by adding 1 cup of water to 10 cups of the glaze mixture. Add more—up to 1 cup per 6 cups of glaze—if it still seems too thick. Experiment with different mixtures on your practice wall. When you find exactly the right formula for your job, mix up twice as much glaze than you think you'll need. If you run short, your second batch will never match your first, ruining the effect.

1. **Load the sponge.** Fill your application tray about one-third full (too much glaze makes the tray harder to handle, invites spills, and can overload the sponge). Dip the sea sponge in the tray three times: dippy, dippy, dippy. Then tap the sponge three times on a flat surface to remove any excess: tappy, tappy, tappy. I like to use a roller tray as my applicator tray so I can tap the sponge on the rake of the tray, automatically recycling excess glaze.

2. **Wash the wall with the sea sponge.** Use swirling motions, working on a 3- to 4-foot square of wall at a time. Don't lift the sponge from the wall. Instead imagine you're washing it, not painting it, and gently rub the surface. If the glaze seems a bit hard to work, add a little fabric softener to the mix—not a lot, just a touch—to improve flow. The texture of the sea sponge adds character to the effect.

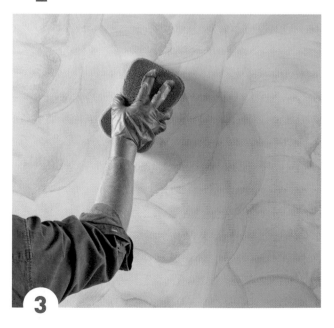

3. **Blot the wall with a synthetic sponge.** Put down the sea sponge and pick up a synthetic sponge. I use a tile sponge because it's large, very absorbent, and rinses out well. Dampen the tile sponge, then gently blot the wall to break up the uniformity of the surface and create highlight and shadow.

4. **Continue to blot randomly,** rotating your wrist to change the aspect angle of the sponge using an "opening and closing the door" motion. Don't swirl or twist the sponge when it is in contact with the surface during this step: twist, blot, remove the sponge from the surface, then repeat the sequence.

5. **Pull the sponge downward over the surface.** Depending on the degree of subtlety you're looking for, the blotted wall may seem a bit blotchy and high-contrast. If that's the case, blend and smooth the surface by pulling a clean, damp tile sponge down the wall as though you're creating a strié effect, which will help even out the tone.

6. **Flip the sponge over and continue.** When one side of the sponge becomes loaded with glaze, flip it over and continue with the other side. As with sponge finishing, the trick is to know when the sponge is approaching the saturation point where the effect will be degraded, and to flip the sponge BEFORE you reach that point. Exactly when is something you can learn only by practice and careful observation, so just like other faux effects, first experiment on a practice wall. If all else fails, completely remove the wash using a clean sponge and a bucket of clean water, wait for the wall to dry, and start again!

tips 'n' tricks

Experiment, but don't go overboard. Working with a wash is like painting with watercolors—you only have so much control. Remember, this effect is about creating an inconsistent surface, so don't try to make it look uniform. Sometimes I even spritz the surface lightly with a water bottle to further dilute the pigment and add to the weathered look. On the other hand, don't fuss with the effect all day. You must know when to walk away, and that's something experience will teach you.

TIPS, TRICKS, TOOLS, and More . . .

Some painting, cleanup, storage, and disposal tips are summarized here for easy reference. For more on cleaning and storage, see chapter 6.

Painting like a pro

Instead of lugging around a gallon of glaze, fill a 1-quart dishsoap bottle. The bottle has an air-tight seal, it's easy to control, you can squeeze out just the amount you need, and most importantly, if you drop it, you won't get glaze all over everything!

Even Wall Wizards have a hard time knowing what color is inside a nondescript can of paint. Dab the paint on the outside of the can. To make it easier to match the color when you touch up a room, dab a paint spot on the backside of a switch plate in the room and write the color name, number, and manufacturer on it.

If you hate paint drips and splatters on your eyeglasses, cover them with plastic kitchen cling wrap. When splatters happen, simply remove the old and apply a new piece.

A transport tray makes it easier to move around the room and paint. To make your own, cover a TV tray with about 15 sheets of aluminum foil. Squeeze the paint or glaze onto the aluminum foil and load your tool from that puddle. When the paint starts to dry and get sticky, or if you need to blend another color, all you have to do is peel away the top layer for a clean surface.

To paint wall switches and vent covers, wash them thoroughly and coat them with a white-pigmented sealer, such as Kilz, let dry, then paint with the finish color.

Clamp a hair clip to a sponge to create the perfect handle. Clips are made of plastic so they're easy to clean; they make the sponge ergonomic so that it's easier to hold; and they make it simple to control the sponge during application.

To create a crisp line between the wall and the ceiling when cutting in, apply a light strip of lip balm around the edge of the ceiling. The paint won't stick to the wax in the lip balm, and there is no need to remove it after the paint is dry. (Lip balm also works well as a mask on windows; see page 27.)

You can clean water-based paint from brushes and paint pads in 10 seconds. Here's how:

1. Remove excess paint from the brush or pad.

2. Add ½ cup of fabric softener per gallon of water. Mix several gallons.

3. Dip a brush into the mixture, swish briskly through the water, and count to 10.

4. Dry the brush using a paintbrush spinner. Spin the brush in a wet waste bucket. Rub the tool dry with a small towel.

Have you heard about wrapping paintbrushes in foil and storing them in the freezer? That's a horrible idea! Water-based paint is ruined in freezing conditions; nylon bristles become brittle and break; and a wet wooden handle will crack.

Before applying any paint that has been stored for more than a month, smell it. A mildew or earthy smell indicates there's mold growing in the paint, which will inhibit proper application. Then check the paint's consistency. If it is more viscous than new paint, part of its ingredients have evaporated and the paint is no longer usable. If it appears unusually thin or runny, it means that the paint has separated. Old paint has a tendency to separate into its component parts; once it does so, it is difficult to obtain the same bonding properties. Dispose of it properly.

Dispose of oil or solvent-soaked rags safely and permanently. Fill a clean, 1-gallon metal paint can two-thirds with a 50-50 mixture of water and liquid fabric softener. Stuff the rags in the can, seal it with a metal lid, and take the filled can to a hazardous waste disposal center.

To store paint, place a piece of plastic garbage bag over the top of a paint can. Gently tap the lid closed over the plastic, using a rubber mallet. Store the paint can upside down to keep air from seeping into the can and to prevent a skin from forming. See page 162.

chapter 6

Clean and Store

Admit it—you'd rather toss your tools than go through the rigmarole of proper cleanup, storage, and disposal. It's not that you're lazy; it's just that when a project is complete, you want all the stuff to go away, right? Ignoring a problem isn't going to solve it. If you continually maintain your tools and work area, your painting experience and results will be much better. In this chapter, you complete the painting cycle by understanding the why behind the how-tos of cleaning, washout, storage, and disposal.

By the way, would you like to learn how to clean a brush in 10 seconds or less, without throwing it away? Read on.

CLEAN as You Go

Cleanup is not the last thing you do; it's what you do throughout your paint project. For starters, it's easier to wipe up wet paint than it is to chisel dry paint off a surface. Here are some more helpful tips:

- Maintain your workspace. Centralize the tools in one area. Place them on your project table so you can find them throughout the job.

- Wipe down, sweep, and vacuum frequently so debris will not settle into the surface finish.

- Cleanup any paint splatters or spills immediately. It is easier to clean up wet paint or glaze than it is to chisel it off after it has hardened.

- Set up a large, lined trash can in a convenient location. Constantly pick up and throw away used masking tape, plastic wraps, and other debris as you work. Having a messy workspace prolongs the job and makes it more dangerous.

Clean works!

Teamwork also applies to the final phase of your painting project.

Divide to conquer. Identify, define, and divide the various tasks into logical and manageable steps. Working in a team of two makes the job twice as fast and half as tedious, saving you energy, time, and money.

Stay focused. Stick to your assigned role and task. Clean from the ceiling down, working down and out of the room.

Be thorough. Observe and repeat procedures to ensure quality control.

Reassemble the room

Once the work is finished and the paint has dried, remove all the coverings and clean the room again. Remount all the switch plates, towel bars, drapery hardware, vents, and grills. Turn the power back on at the circuit breaker panel. And, finally, take a moment to admire your handy work and enjoy the beautiful colors and finishes. But not too long; you've got more cleanup to do.

cool tool

Just because a brush and roller spinner is so much fun to play with doesn't mean it's not a practical tool. In fact, this tool cuts drying time for brushes and paint rollers to about one minute. Simply push your brush or paint roller into the spinner, pump the handle, and voila! The water is eliminated from the bristles or roller.

1

2

3

4

Total TOOL Care

Taking care of brushes, rollers, and pads will save you time, energy, and money. Don't throw your tools in a bucket or sink and expect them to clean themselves; they'll be ruined, and you'll end up throwing them away and buying new ones. A Wall Wizard knows: It's no pain to maintain. Clean your brushes every two hours while working with water-based paint and at the end of your project.

Wash out water-based materials

Here's how you can clean water-based paint from brushes and paint pads in 10 seconds:

1. Remove excess paint from the brush or pad by scraping it with the edge of a 10-in-1 tool or the teeth of a brush-cleaning tool.

2. Mix up several gallons of this magic potion in a 5-gallon bucket: For every gallon of warm water, add ½ cup of fabric softener. The fabric softener is a surfactant—it actually makes the water wetter, so it can more easily dissolve paint.

3. Dip your brush into the mixture, swish briskly through the water, and count to 10. The paint will release from the bristles and settle to the bottom of the bucket.

4. To dry your paintbrush quickly, use a paintbrush spinner to fling water from the brush. Spin the brush in a wet waste bucket. To make one, start with an empty 5-gallon plastic bucket with lid. Cut an 8-inch hole in the center of the lid. Place a plastic trash bag in the bucket and snap on the lid. The lid keeps the splatter inside the bucket; toss the bag when finished. Rub the tool dry with a small towel.

Don't clean the brush with dish soap; it will gum up the ferrule and bristles. And there's no need to rinse the tool in fresh water. The more often you clean it with the softener solution, the better it gets. Fabric softener coats the handle, ferrule, and bristles, allowing paint to flow effortlessly off the tool. Magical!

Follow the same steps for rollers and paint pads. Rollers take a little more time, about 30 seconds, and they might require multiple dippings.

When you're done cleaning, don't pour the washout water down the drain! Instead, put a secure lid on the bucket so you can use it again next time you paint. You can use the same cleanout mixture for several days—even for several different paint jobs with different color paint. Use the mixture until you notice a film of paint starting to develop on the top of the water. Then dispose of this washout water using the cat-litter method (see page 165).

Removing oil-based paints

This cleaning method effectively strips oil-based materials from paintbrush bristles. Follow the steps carefully to avoid damaging the brush. You'll need about 20 seconds to clean oil-based paints from a brush, about 30 seconds from a roller.

If you wash out your expensive china-bristle brushes in mineral spirits, they will become stiff due to paint residues left inside the bristles. This multistep washout technique breaks down the oil-based paint and conditions the brush.

1. Start with three clean glass jars (such as mayonnaise jars) with lids that have a seal. Fill jar #1 about two-thirds full of mineral spirits. Fill jar #2 with a 50-50 solution of mineral spirits and denatured alcohol. Fill jar #3 with pure denatured alcohol. Mark each jar. If you are cleaning paint rollers, paint pads, or other tools that won't fit into the jars, use lidded buckets.

2. Scrape off excess paint using the edge of a 10-in-1 tool.

3. Dip the brush into jar #1 and swish it around for about 10 seconds. This is the "hottest" solution and will remove about 70 percent of the paint from the tool. Use a brush and roller spinner to spin the excess out of the brush into an empty bucket.

4. Dip the brush into jar #2, swish it around for about 10 seconds, then remove and spin. The mineral spirits dissolve the binders; the alcohol begins to strip out the oils. This will remove about 20 percent more.

5. Dip the brush in jar #3, swish for 10 seconds, remove, and spin. At this point, the natural oils have been stripped from the bristles, leaving them brittle and open, so they must be reconditioned.

6. Finish by swishing the brush for about 10 seconds in the liquid fabric softener mixture made following the recipe on the previous page. This neutralizes the alcohol and conditions the bristles by restoring their oils. Rub the tool dry with a small towel.

tips 'n' tricks

We all have one—a mucked-up water-based tool that wasn't cleaned properly before it was put away. Here's how to resurrect that old brush so it looks and works as good as new. Mix equal parts water, ammonia, and liquid fabric softener in a glass baking pan. Lay the brush in the mixture for 24 to 36 hours. Take it out and scrub off any stubborn paints. Finish by using the water-based washout method. Repeat until the brush is clean and then store it properly. For a quick solution, use spray oven cleaner; the lye will dissolve the old paint. The most extreme way to clean a tool is to use lacquer thinner, but use this powerful solvent carefully and sparingly.

Cleaning roller covers

When you are finished painting, clean the excess paint from the roller cover using the curved edge of a 10-in-1 tool. Follow the directions for cleaning water-based or oil-based paint given on the preceding pages. Don't forget to use the brush and roller spinner: Notice that the tines on the end of the spinner are the same diameter as the inside of the roller cover. Slide the cover off the roller frame and onto the spinner, and dip and spin until paint is removed, as with brushes.

Disposable paint rollers

I admit it: Disposable roller covers are more convenient for some jobs. To pull it off the frame, put the roller inside a plastic bag, grab the cover through the bag, pull it off, then seal the bag for disposal. Clean the roller frame appropriately for the type of paint you used. Oil the frame with a little spray lubricant and hang it up.

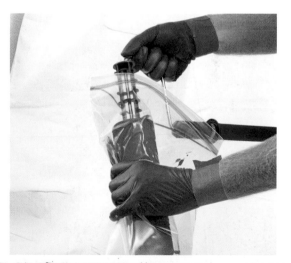

tips 'n' tricks

Don't waste the excess paint in your roller pan. Clean out your old shoe polish bottles really well (cleaning the sponge applicator thoroughly as well), drop in a glass marble or a stainless steel nut (that's the agitator), cap it, label it with the room, paint, and wall color, and store it upside down in the nearest closet. It'll last up to ten years. That way, if you get a nick or scrape in a wall, you just shake the container and sponge over the scratch. Clean the sponge head again after use.

STORAGE Solutions

Proper storage preserves the investment you've made in paint and tools, and it makes it easier to find everything you need when it's time to begin a new paint project.

Storing paint

To store your paint so it lasts a lifetime, follow these steps:

1. If a paint can is less than one-half full, transfer excess paint to a smaller container. The storage rule is no more than one-third air space to two-thirds liquid. You can purchase gallon- and quart-size metal paint cans from a home supply store. Pour the paint through a nylon stocking to strain it. Label where you bought the paint, its type, color, sheen, mix number, and the storage date.

2. Using a plastic bag, cut a circle 1 inch larger than the diameter of the paint can. This plastic circle will serve as a gasket to prevent moisture in the paint from corroding the lid of the can. It also plugs the holes that you punched in the can rim earlier. Most importantly, when you open the can to reuse the paint, you can easily scrape the pigments that have settled on the plastic back into the can.

3. Apply nonstick vegetable spray to one side of the plastic. It lubricates the rim, seals the lid, and prevents a skin from forming on the paint.

4. This step sounds odd, but it is essential in storing paint: Breathe into the can three times. The carbon dioxide from your breath forces out oxygen that is left in the can. Remember Painting Law 3: The enemy of paint is air (or oxygen, to be more specific).

5. Place the plastic gasket over the top of the paint can, sprayed side down. Gently tap the lid closed using a rubber mallet, which is less likely to deform the lid or rim. Tap the lid flush with the rim. Place a rag over the can before striking to prevent splatters.

6. Store the paint can upside down to keep air from seeping into the can and to prevent a skin from forming. Store paint about 18 inches off the floor in a room, such as a basement, where the temperature averages about 50 degrees year-round. Keep paint locked away from children and never store it near a source of ignition, such as a pilot light or open flame. Both latex and oil-based paints can explode—I've seen it happen.

Storing paintbrushes

It's not enough just to clean brushes; you should also store them properly to keep the bristles from being damaged. The best and easiest way I know is to slip the dry brush back into its original plastic or cardboard cover. If you threw away the cover, you can make another one from light cardboard. Measure around the ferrule of the brush and add about 3 inches. Cut a piece of cardboard that wide and slightly longer than the distance from the top of the ferrule to the end of the bristles. Wrap the cardboard loosely around the brush and tape it. Slide the brush inside.

If you are as organized as I am, you can even color-code the brush covers. I use red for oil-based china-bristle brushes and blue for water-based latex brushes. Finally, hang your paintbrush to store it—that's what the hole in the handle is for!

wizard WARNING

Have you heard about wrapping paintbrushes in foil and storing them in the freezer? That's a horrible idea! Water-based paint is ruined in freezing conditions; nylon bristles become brittle and break; and a wet wooden handle will crack. If you want to store brushes temporarily during a paint project, wrap them in plastic so the paint and bristles are completely covered. Properly clean brushes for long-term storage.

Storing rollers and pads
PAINT ROLLERS

After roller covers have been spun and dried, the best way to store them is to put them back on the roller frame and hang the roller handle from a nail. That way, the roller is suspended in midair so the cover will dry evenly and hold its shape.

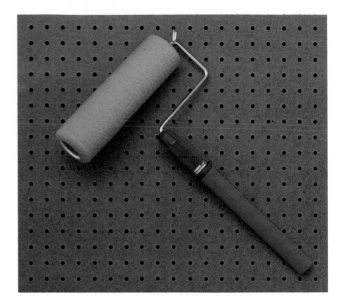

PAINT PADS

Some pads are good only for two or three applications, others may last longer—it all depends on the quality of the pad and the nature of the surface on which it was used. Inspect the pads before storing and discard any that show wear (retain the handle and buy a new pad for your next job). To keep the pads fluffy, store them bristle side up.

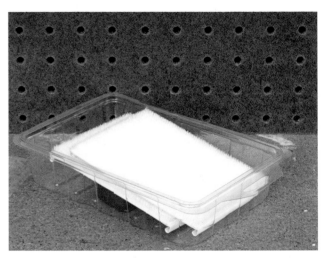

quiz the WIZ

Can I save the paint I poured out of the can?

Absolutely, but don't just pour it back into the can from your bucket. Stretch a piece of nylon stocking over the opening of the can to strain any contaminates that dropped into the paint or were carried to it by your brush. Throw away the stocking when finished.

How can you tell if paint is no longer good?

Many factors can damage paint. Air contamination causes paint to dry and rust particles to form in the can. Unsatisfactory environmental conditions break the binders that help the paint adhere to a surface. Heat actually "cooks" the paint. Water-based paint that's been frozen undergoes a chemical change that can impede its bonding ability, breaking down the color pigments. Typically it is difficult to salvage paint that has gone bad.

Before applying any paint that's been stored for more than a month, smell it. A mildew or earthy smell indicates there's mold growing in the paint, which will inhibit proper application. Then check the paint's consistency. If it is more viscous than new paint, part of its ingredients have evaporated and the paint is no longer usable. If it appears unusually thin or runny, it means that the paint has separated. Old paint has a tendency to separate into its component parts; once it does, it is difficult to obtain the same bonding properties. Dispose of it properly.

The Dish on DISPOSAL

Paint products and latex paint washout water are not as hazardous as they once were, but they still require special disposal. An ounce of paint poured onto the ground can contaminate as much as 12 cubic feet of soil. The best solution for paint and solvent disposal is to take the materials to a local hazardous waste disposal site where they can be recycled. Some sites even feature swap shops where you can pick up free painting materials that others have dropped off. Search under hazardous waste in directories.

If you must dispose of these materials yourself, never pour them down the drain, into a storm sewer, onto the ground, or throw them into the trash. The secret is to convert paint products from a liquid state to a dry condition. In this case, Wizards work dry. Here's how to dispose of paint and solvents correctly, minimizing their impact on the environment:

Take a 5-gallon bucket, line it with a trash compactor bag. Fill the bucket half full with crystalline cat litter, and pour your clean-up water and excess paint into the can. Lift the bag out and twist-tie it shut. Set the bag aside for several days, or until the contents becomes a solid mass, then throw the bag in the trash. Leave the lids off empty latex paint cans until the paint residue inside dries and then toss the buckets into the trash.

tips 'n' tricks

Instead of disposing of leftover paint at the dump, donate it to your local high school or college drama department; they can often make use of your paints in scene construction. Community centers or neighborhood housing organizations might also take such donations.

Oil-based solvents

Oil-based solvents can be stored and used for years if sealed and stored properly. Solvents such as paint thinners can be refreshed and reused repeatedly, and that's good for the environment and for your wallet.

When solvents rest undisturbed for several days, they will separate by their chemical makeup, specific density, and material composition. Because the materials in paint will settle to the bottom, the solvents will clarify on top. When the paint materials fill the containers about half way, pour off the clear solvent for reuse. When the bottle is half-full, scrape the residue out of the bottle and dispose of it in cat litter as described on the previous page. Wipe out the jars and reuse them for further cleanup jobs. If you have any questions about waste disposal, contact your local solid waste disposal office about safely disposing of or recycling leftover paint, used paint buckets, petroleum-based solvents, and other materials.

For safety, mobility, and long-term storage, place the glass jars in a large plastic storage bin with lid. Mark the bin with red duct tape and write "CAUTION—Oil-based Washout Storage Container—CAUTION" across the tape so there is no mistaking what it is. Tightly pack crumpled newspapers around the glass jars to absorb spills and to

prevent glass breakage. After using the container, tightly close the jars, allow the newspaper to dry out from any spills, and close up the storage container. Store it in a cool, dry, and secure place.

wizard WARNING

Dispose of oil or solvent-soaked rags safely and permanently. Fill a clean, 1-gallon metal paint can two-thirds full with a 50-50 mixture of water and liquid fabric softener. Stuff the rags in the can, seal it with a metal lid, and take the filled can to a hazardous waste disposal center. The water deprives the rags of the oxygen needed to spontaneously combust, and the fabric softener breaks the bonds of the oils and solvents, making them less volatile.

Never store solvent-soaked materials indoors. They release harmful fumes and can easily catch fire.

Proper storage of tools and materials protects your investment in them and sets the stage for an easy start and successful finish to your next painting project.

chapter 7

Wallpapering

Welcome to the magic of pattern and the power of texture! Nothing gives a room more aesthetic appeal with less effort and technical skill than wallpaper. Wallpaper can enhance your home's architecture and give your home a shot of color and design in any style and palette you can imagine. Along with paint and faux finishes, wallpaper should play an important part in your design choices.

Although not as inexpensive as paint and glaze, wallpaper is also among the most affordable ways to achieve a complete design transformation. A few bolts of wallpaper cost considerably less than a new suite of furniture, bath fixtures, or kitchen appliances. Wallpaper is one of the most practical, accessible—and overlooked—ways of creating design and dimension in your home. Wallpaper can complement paint and faux finishes to create a complete decorating statement.

This chapter will show you how to select and apply wallpaper to create drama and beauty anywhere in your house. I'll introduce you to the materials, tools, and techniques that will help you achieve decorating success. In my 25 years of teaching how to apply wallpaper, it has become apparent that fear of the process keeps homeowners from taking advantage of the decorating power of wallpaper. That's understandable: The techniques can seem daunting, especially if they have never been explained to you. But if you follow the steps in this chapter, you will be able to realize the joy that can come from creating an artful and expressive home interior.

The MATERIAL World

Wallpaper is available in five common materials, each with its own characteristics.

● **Vinyl-coated** materials have a washable or scrubbable vinyl coating applied to the surface, either as an ingredient in the inks that create the pattern or as a clear coating over the top of a pattern, much like the clear coat on a car or the varnish on a hardwood floor. Vinyl-coated materials offer an ideal combination of price, stability, and ease of use.

● **Vinyl-laminated** materials are made of two layers: an outer layer of vinyl that has the pattern printed on it and a substrate, or paper backing, that adheres to the wall. They are easy to strip—you simply grab the vinyl layer and pull the whole layer off at once, as the adhesive that holds the vinyl layer to the paper layer is weaker than the adhesive that holds the paper layer to the wall. Then you strip the paper substrate separately, which is relatively easy because the paper has no ink or vinyl coating on it and readily absorbs stripping solution. Vinyl-laminated materials have largely been abandoned by the industry because they've become too cost-prohibitive for the market and are hard to find, although a few patterns are still available. They are very washable, so if you can find one, it would be great for a bath or kitchen.

● **Solid vinyl** is one solid sheet of vinyl that's extruded, colored, and applied to cheesecloth backing to which the adhesive can bond. Generally these are either nonpatterned or random-patterned and are scrubbable and extremely durable. Solid-vinyl wallpaper is installed frequently in large commercial buildings such as hotels and convention centers.

● **Naturals** are organic materials such as grass cloth, cork, or bamboo that are laminated to a heavy paper backing for stability. Natural materials tend to be expensive, and most are not washable, but they create an effect that you simply can't get with a printed material.

● **Untrimmed** materials date back to the 1400s, when patterns were printed on paper stock using hand-cut wooden blocks. Up to 30 different colors might be used to create a single design. You can still buy a few historic patterns made with this material. They're costly and most often used in historic restoration projects. These papers require hand-trimming before applying.

nonwovens

The wallpaper of the future is beginning to hit the market. Nonwoven materials are infused with an adhesive on one side and a pattern on the other. A single sheet includes the adhesive, the backing, the decorative face, the pattern, and the washable surface all in one. These materials are extremely washable and durable. The pattern penetrates into the surface of the material, giving a dimensional quality that conventionally printed wallpapers don't have. The adhesives penetrate the base material, creating a consistency of adhesion. They are also 100 percent strippable: If you don't like the pattern in five years, you can grab it and pull everything off the wall in one swoop—pattern, substrate, adhesive, and all. Nonwovens are also very stable materials, so seams stay straight and are virtually invisible.

Anatomy of a Wallpaper BOOK

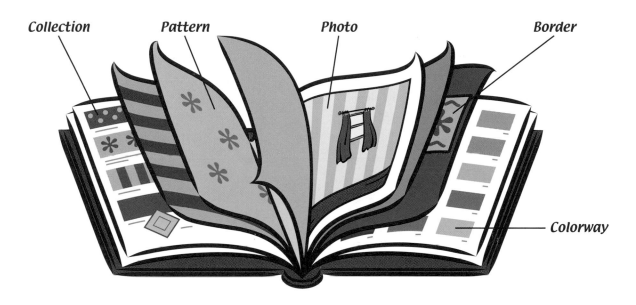

Collection   Pattern   Photo   Border

Colorway

Collection: Everything offered in a given book.

Pattern: The basic graphic design of the wallpaper.

Colorway: The colors in which the pattern is executed. One pattern is often available in many different colorways.

Complementary materials and effects: Borders, wainscoting, and murals that coordinate with different wallpaper patterns. These are designed to enhance or complement the main pattern. They also can stand on their own: You can use a wallpaper border, for instance, as a frieze (a decorative border) at the top of a painted wall.

Vignette Photography: Photographs of the wallpaper installed in studio settings that bring the material to life in a homelike environment.

wizard WARNING

When you find a wallpaper you like in a book, you usually order it through the dealer to be delivered to your home by mail or express service. Orders often arrive in three to five days. But before you set a date for applying the wallpaper—or book a wallpaper contractor's time—make sure the material isn't back-ordered and that it will arrive before you need it.

Using the book

When you consider a sample in a wallpaper book, hold it vertically. That's how the material will be applied to the wall, and many materials will not look right viewed any other way. Slowly change the angle of a wallpaper book and you will probably see colors change, textures become more or less evident, and sheen and contrast vary. So it's important to view the material as it will be installed in your room, particularly with moiré or refractory patterns. After the pattern is printed, these materials are embossed with a texture that acts like a prism to reflect light in a specific manner. This quality is called *visual luster*.

Once you've narrowed your selection, ask if you can take the book—or a cut sample of the product—to the room where you're planning to apply it. Attach the sample to the wall with pushpins or blue painter's tape and look at it in morning, midday, afternoon, and evening light, and by artificial light. If the store has the wallpaper in stock, ask the retailer if you can take one roll home, handle it carefully, retain the labeling and packaging, and return it if you are not happy with this light test.

CHOOSING a Wallpaper

To me, the most difficult part of a wallpapering job is choosing which to use. Seriously, you look at so many patterns and colors it's hard to keep them straight. Wallpaper manufacturers help you in your search by organizing groups of wallpaper into collections. A collection is just that: a number of different patterns, each often executed in several color schemes, along with complementary materials and effects such as borders, wainscoting, and even murals.

Collections are shown at wallpaper retailers in bound volumes called *wallpaper books, sample books,* or simply *collections.* Because the books are costly, and so that there will be enough books available for all customers to review, most wallpaper retailers limit the number of books a customer can take home to study. Some retailers do not allow books to be taken out of the store. Dealers who do loan books will probably require a deposit that is refundable when you return the book. There's also usually a time limit on these loans—often 10 days.

Collections are generally organized into groups, often by room function. These categories help you winnow the vast number of patterns quickly. The categories are simply suggestions, however, and are not designed to limit you. If you see a pattern you like in a living room book and think it would be perfect in your bedroom, go ahead and use it! But be careful what kind of wallpaper you apply to bathroom and kitchen walls—some materials will not stand up to high-moisture, high-traffic areas.

SYMBOLS: International performance symbols like these often appear in wallpaper books and on product labels.

Symbol	Label	Symbol	Label
∼	Spongeable		Nonpasted
≈	Washable		Paste-the-wall
≋	Extra washable		Random match
≅	Scrubbable		Straight match
	Moderate light fastness		Drop match
	Good light fastness	$\frac{50}{25}$ cm	The repeat
	Strippable	↑	Direction
	Peelable	↓↑	Reverse hanging
	Prepasted		

Repeat

Repeat is the distance between like elements of the design. Repeat differs from scale (see next page) but is just as important. Whether a pattern has a short or long repeat is in itself neither good nor bad—suitability depends upon the room, how it will be furnished, and what effect you want to achieve.

Line

Pattern repeats create lines in the wallpaper (except for solid-color wallpapers with no pattern or texture). Some lines are obvious, as in a vertical stripe pattern, and others are subtle, as in a floral or damask pattern. To see even the most subtle lines, stand back from the pattern and relax your eyes' focus. You may see vertical lines, horizontal lines, diagonal lines, or all three, depending on the pattern. Line is an important design element because your eye tends to follow a line. If the vertical line in the pattern is strongest, it can make a room seem taller. A horizontal line can make a room seem wider or longer; a diagonal line can make a room seem larger in every dimension.

Straight match

Drop match

Random match

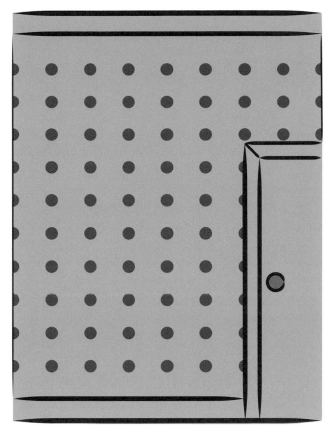

Small

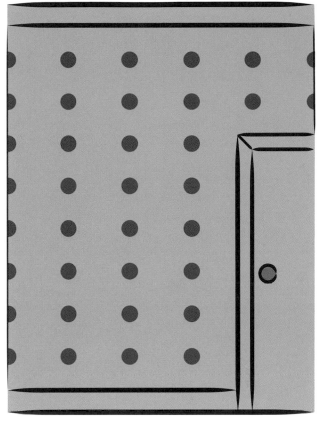

Medium

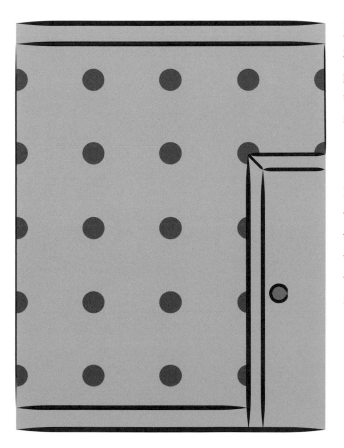

Large

Scale

Scale is the size of the dominant element in the wallpaper's pattern. Other factors being equal, designs of large scale tend to be more dramatic and those of a smaller scale are more intimate.

Proportion

Proportion is the ratio of the size of the dominant element within the wallpaper's pattern to the size of the room in which it's installed. Consider the pattern and judge how it will look in the room—whether the pattern is so large it will overwhelm a small room or so small it will appear busy in a large one.

Straight match

➡|⬅

tips 'n' tricks

MEASURE THE GRID

Take a framing square and run it across the wallpaper pattern.

Measure the distance between repeats—identical parts of the design.

That measurement determines the grid, and gives you a mathematical definition of the design's scale. Once you know that number, you can easily compare the relative scale of different patterns.

GRID

GRID stands for **G**reater **R**hythm **I**n **D**esign, an acronym I coined long ago. It has since been adopted by the wallpaper industry to describe the interaction of scale, repeat, and line. Step back from an installed wallpaper, blur your focus, and you can see a literal grid in the design—intersecting horizontal, vertical, and at times diagonal lines that make up the wallpaper's metapattern, the big pattern behind all the smaller design elements. Ultimately it's GRID that determines the effect of the wallpaper in a given room, and the term provides an easy way to talk about all the elements of a wallpaper in one word.

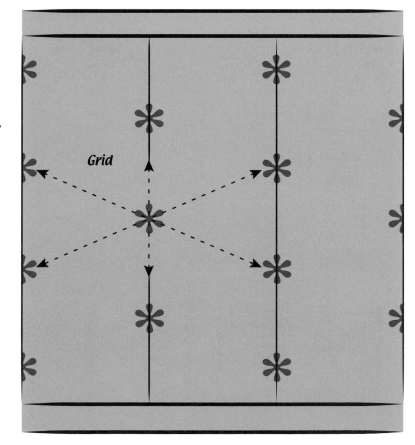

Drop match

➡|⬅

Anatomy of a BOLT

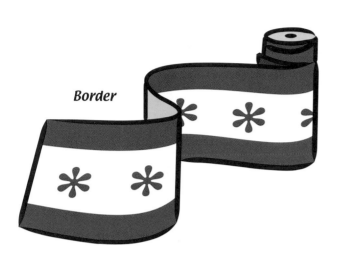

Border

A bolt is a continuous length of wallpaper rolled for convenient handling. There are two standard bolt sizes:

European Standard Bolts (Euro rolls) are 20½ inches wide and about 35 feet long and cover approximately 56 gross square feet (not including pattern repeat, and pattern waste, and usage length). (Note that Euro rolls are actually measured in metric.)

American Standard Bolts are approximately 27 inches wide and about 33 feet long and cover approximately 72 gross square feet (not including pattern repeat and pattern waste).

Specialty bolts

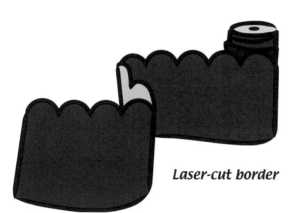

Laser-cut border

● **Borders** usually range from 2 to 28 inches wide and are 15 feet long. Borders can also be packaged in a single continuous roll cut to a length you special order. They can be either straight runs with parallel edges or what's referred to as scallop- or laser-cut borders (left).

● **Natural materials,** such as grass cloth, are usually 36 inches wide and 24 feet long and cover about 72 gross square feet. Because natural materials tend to have grain, like wood, rather than the pattern of printed wallpaper, the greater width is designed to create more of a panel effect—similar to wood paneling—than a pattern effect.

tips 'n' tricks

Designers have an additional option these days: laser- or die-cut borders. Now they can create a pattern with an irregular edge that overlays the design of the wallpaper underneath, giving a frieze effect. These materials are usually applied directly over the wallpaper with a vinyl-over-vinyl adhesive.

Anatomy of a SHEET

A sheet is the most basic element of a wallpapering job, just as a brick is the most basic element of a brick wall.

Sheet: A length of wallpaper cut to the height of the wall to be covered plus 4 inches.

Key element: The largest obvious graphic element printed on the face of the wallpaper. Some wallpapers such as textures, naturals, and random match designs have no key element, but they do have shade variations.

Pattern repeat: The interval between reoccurrences of the key element, usually 1 to 36 inches.

Backing or substrate: The side of the material on which the adhesive is applied.

Trim-off: The part of the material removed to allow the wallpaper to fit the wall.

Border: A narrow strip of wallpaper that complements the main design.

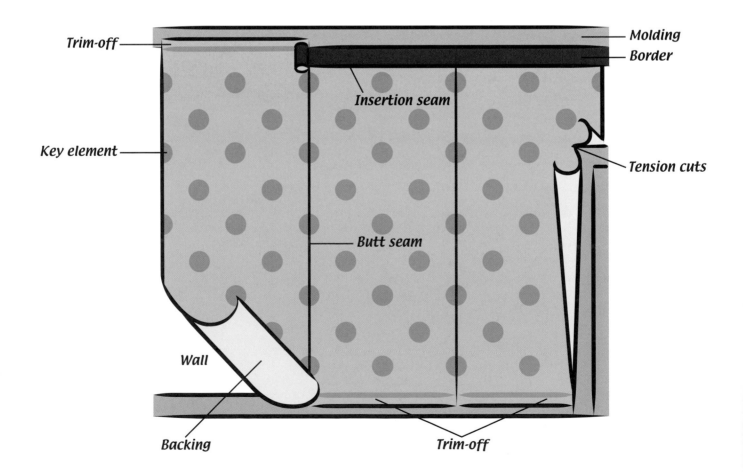

Same pattern, same place

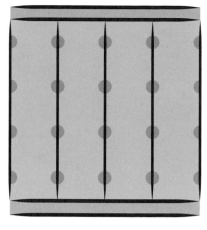

Straight match: The pattern lines up horizontally.

Every other sheet matches

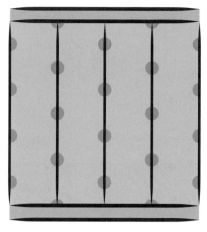

Drop match: The pattern lines up diagonally as well as horizontally.

Reverse-hanging for shading

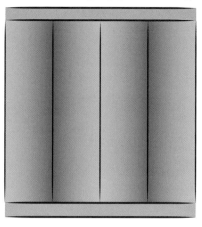

Random match: Pattern elements do not align horizontally or diagonally.

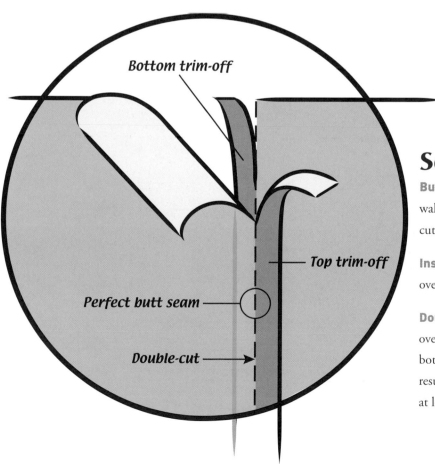

Bottom trim-off

Top trim-off

Perfect butt seam

Double-cut

Seams

Butt seam: Where two sheets of wallpaper meet edge to edge without cutting or trimming.

Insertion seam: Where two materials overlap, such as a border and a wallpaper.

Double-cut seam: Where two sheets overlap and a single cut is made through both layers. The trim-off is removed, resulting in a perfect butt seam as shown at left.

HOW MANY Rolls to Buy

Wallpaper is priced and measured by the single roll, although it comes packaged in double- or triple-roll bolts. Remember this as you figure out how much wallpaper to buy.

Today most wallpapers come in Euro rolls, which hold about 25 percent less material than American rolls. However, most natural materials, such as grass cloth, cork, bamboo, and burlap, are sold by the American roll. Determine whether the material you are buying is measured in Euro (metric) rolls or American (nonmetric) rolls. Then estimate the number of rolls to buy as follows:

Multiply the perimeter of the room (the length of all walls added together) by the height of the room (the distance from floor to ceiling, including moldings, if any). The result is the gross square footage of the walls. If you'll be applying Euro rolls and the ceilings are less than 9 feet high, divide the gross square footage by 25—the number of usable square feet in a Euro roll. If the room is taller than 9 feet, divide by 23.5. This lower number accounts for the added height of the room and increased pattern repeat usage in the roll.

If you are buying American rolls, divide the gross square footage by 27 for rooms less than 9 feet tall, divide by 25.5 for rooms more than 9 feet tall. Don't deduct any square footage for doors and windows; that helps to ensure you have enough material to account for trimming waste, pattern repeat, and pattern match.

Order at least one more bolt than you think you'll need. You can always return it if you don't use it, but trying to buy more wallpaper later with the same pattern and dye lot can be an exercise in frustration. And if the pattern has been discontinued or the stock of a dye lot exhausted, you'll have to strip what you've already applied and start over. Keep any extra wallpaper on hand for future repairs. It can also be handy for making room embellishments, such as covers for switch plates, heater vent grilles, or even lampshades, wastebaskets, or other decorative features.

how to order border

Borders are packaged in 15-foot or 5-yard lengths, so divide the perimeter of the room in feet by 15 to find the number of border packages you'll need. There's no way of knowing where the pattern starts on each roll, so always order at least one more package than you think you'll need. Order two more packages on larger jobs. That accounts for the amount of usable pattern repeat within each roll—and may even leave you some leftover material to use in creating other decorative effects.

Material estimation

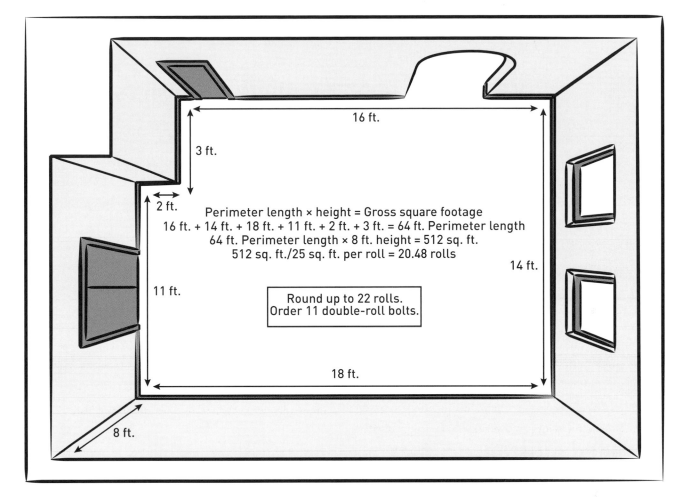

16 ft.

3 ft.

2 ft.

Perimeter length × height = Gross square footage
16 ft. + 14 ft. + 18 ft. + 11 ft. + 2 ft. + 3 ft. = 64 ft. Perimeter length
64 ft. Perimeter length × 8 ft. height = 512 sq. ft.
512 sq. ft./25 sq. ft. per roll = 20.48 rolls

Round up to 22 rolls.
Order 11 double-roll bolts.

14 ft.

11 ft.

18 ft.

8 ft.

quiz the WIZ

When is a roll not a roll?

A **roll** is a unit of measure, just like a foot or a yard. It's not a physical roll of material, in spite of the name. The coiled cylinder of wallpaper material that you buy is called a **bolt,** like a bolt of fabric. Just as a bolt of fabric may contain many yards, a bolt of wallpaper almost always contains more than one roll of wallpaper. Most bolts contain two or three rolls of material in one continuous length. Thus a particular wallpaper that is sold in rolls that are 16 feet long may be packaged as a double-roll bolt, a continuous length 32 feet long rolled into a cylinder. So once you've determined how many rolls you need, find out how many rolls are in a bolt of the pattern you're buying. Then divide the number of rolls in your total by the number of rolls in a bolt to determine the number of packages—bolts—of wallpaper to buy.

The STICKY Stuff

Over the past two decades, there has been a great deal of experimentation with adhesives, some more successful than others. These days your adhesive options have been refined to a tried-and-true few:

Organic adhesives

Usually starch-based, these water-soluble adhesives have good tack, or holding power, but release when saturated, facilitating stripping. Their solubility makes them easy to work with so you can easily clean your tools, worktable, and the inevitable slops and spills. Organic adhesives also won't stain, so they're generally used on very fine papers such as murals and organics that might stain easily if synthetic adhesives are used.

Blended adhesives

These adhesives blend organic and synthetic materials. They have greater bond strength than organic adhesives yet are still relatively easy to clean up.

Synthetic adhesives

Acrylic-based and extremely strong and tacky, synthetics are an excellent choice for use in kitchens, bathrooms, and other high-moisture areas where organic adhesives might fail. A synthetic bond can easily be sheared, making wallpaper applied with this adhesive easily strippable. Adhesive drips and spills are hard to remove from room surfaces, and they're even more tenacious when they dry. Residual adhesive that's dried onto a wall is virtually impossible to remove and can impair surfaces to be painted. Organic or blended adhesives are a better choice in most cases.

quiz the WIZ
Should I use activator?

Activator, the gel-like material that absorbs and holds moisture, has become available in the last 10 years. It's designed to eliminate the need for wetting the wallpaper in a water tray to activate the adhesive. Instead, you roll the activator gel onto the back of the wallpaper. It does work, but it takes more time and energy to roll the stuff onto the wallpaper thoroughly and evenly than to simply dunk the wallpaper in a tray the conventional way. In the Wizard's world, activator is a tedious, tiring, and expensive extra step.

Prepasted wallpaper

Wallpapers with adhesive applied at the factory during the manufacturing process eliminate the need to apply adhesive to the paper during installation. That saves installation time and mess and provides a more consistent bond.

Nonpasted Wallpaper

Some wallpapers need adhesive applied before you install them. Nonpasted wallpaper takes slightly more time to install but allows an experienced wallpaper installer to adjust the amount and consistency of the adhesive to match the porosity of the wall and the wallpaper backing.

Here are the three inviolable precepts of applying wallpaper. They're pretty simple, really. Follow them, and your job will go much more smoothly and, most importantly, you'll get professional results that'll look great when you're done—and for a long time to come.

Every new wall gets a new plumb line.

Using a chalkline and a weight, mark a straight, perfectly vertical line that acts as the starting point on each wall. Aligning the wallpaper seam with the line ensures that the wallpaper is hung straight up and down, no matter how out of square the room itself may be. It also ensures that the alignment of each drop of wallpaper relates to the same standard, regardless of which wall it is applied to. That way there's no distortion of perspective between walls.

Use yellow chalk—blue chalk bleeds through the seams—and lightly brush away excess. Snap the line on the wall, where the right edge of the first sheet will be.

Cut inside corners, wrap outside corners.

2

Walls often are not square to each other, so folding a sheet around an inside corner can cause puckering and introduce crookedness. Outside corners are wrapped to avoid having an exposed cut edge that can lift or tear at the corner. Don't worry about pattern mismatches in inside corners; such a corner is rarely seen closely, so it's a perfect place to make up for out-of-square walls. As I often tell people in my wallpapering seminars, I love corners—they're great for burying any misalignment that may occur in a place no one is likely to notice.

Avoid overlaps.

3

Wallpaper used to be printed with a blank edge that had to be trimmed by hand or installed with an overlap. Now wallpaper comes with precisely trimmed edges that are designed to be butted tightly against one another in order to create matching patterns and invisible seams. There are a few more reasons not to create overlaps: Wallpaper doesn't stick to wallpaper well—it is designed to adhere to the wall itself, and overlapped seams will come loose. Overlaps also stretch and stress the material, which can shrink and ruin the seam match as it dries. Finally overlaps create highly visible ridges or bumps in the finish, which ruin the effect.

The Henry Ford METHOD

I'm going to introduce you to a better way to install wallpaper. I call it the Henry Ford method. Henry Ford created a production line that could build 43 cars in the time his competitors could build one. I'll show you how to do the same thing when installing wallpaper. Rather than trying to do several operations at once, you'll plan the job first, prepare the wallpaper for installation second, and install it third. Wizards plan ahead, then act with confidence.

I've broken down each operation into easy-to-follow steps that group like tasks. You'll do all the cutting, then all the trimming, and finally all the installing. The result: You'll be able to complete your job in one-third the time or less. And once you've gotten the hang of the work (so to speak), it's a lot less stressful and chaotic than installing wallpaper sheet by sheet, and it results in a much higher quality, more professional-looking job.

It all starts with a well-planned layout that shows where each sheet will go on the walls. Here's an essential point: Layout and installation are two entirely different processes.

● Layout is foreseeing what the installation will look like: where each sheet will go, where each seam will fall, how the wallpaper's pattern, if there is one, will be placed on the wall.

● Installation is the process of installing the wallpaper in the room in accordance with the layout you've planned.

If you start applying the wallpaper before you've settled on a layout, you almost certainly will end up with awkward seam locations, strips of wallpaper too narrow for proper adhesion, pattern mismatches in conspicuous places, or a strong wallpaper pattern that feels out of balance with the room's focal point. To avoid such problems, follow the four planning principles explained on the next page: They are not laws; they're guidelines.

process vs. product

The product reflects the process. If you have the process down, the result looks great. So bear with me for a moment while we go over how we get the job done right. I'm about to show you a great bag of Wizard tricks that may seem complex now, but they'll ultimately make the process go much more smoothly. The result: fantastic walls!

The four planning principles

1. **Create a trial layout** that starts at the vertical centerline of the room's focal point wall (I'll talk more about how to identify this wall on page 191). From this starting point the layout will show you where seams will fall across this wall and around the room.

2. **Put the last seam, which usually mismatches, in a dead corner**—the most inconspicuous spot in the room. Common dead corners include behind doors, the header space above the entrance, and hidden alcoves.

3. **Reduce the number of full-length seams** by planning or adjusting the layout to place some seams within windows and doors.

4. **Try to leave half a sheet**—or at the very least a strip no narrower than 6 inches—beside a door or window.

The overall goal is to minimize the seams and maximize the width of each sheet.

Remember, these guidelines are not absolute. Sometimes you'll need to make compromises based on the room's dimensions, the wallpaper pattern repeat, the location of doors, windows, moldings, and corners, and other factors that won't become apparent until you've finished your layout. The first trial layout you develop may not satisfy all of these principles. Consider it a first draft and keep applying the principles, making adjustments and compromises, until you're satisfied that your seam placements work best in the room you're working in. Sometimes, instead of making alterations and adjustments to your original layout, you might want to try several layouts, each beginning at a different point, to see which works best. This may seem like a delay in the process, but it is much easier to make changes to your layout with pencil and paper than after you've applied (or misapplied) sheets of wallpaper to the wall.

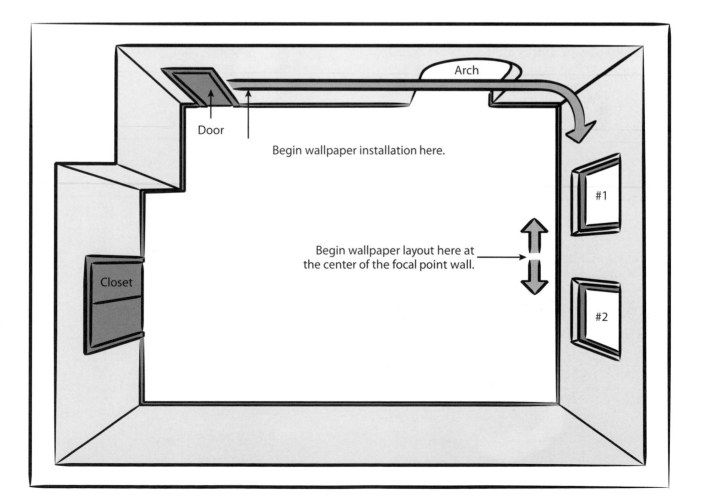

Arch

Door

Begin wallpaper installation here.

Closet

#1

Begin wallpaper layout here at the center of the focal point wall.

#2

My Mistake

DOUBLE YOUR FUN!

Here's something they don't tell you on the package: When you're installing wallpaper on a ceiling, always double-paste!

I once was working in a small bathroom where the client had specified using the same wallpaper on the ceiling as on the walls. The effect can be quite dramatic, especially in a small room.

This time the installation was dramatic. I'd done all the proper preparation, and meticulously too. It pays to be picky in bathrooms, as soap, makeup, and other residues can build up on the walls and wreak havoc with a wallpaper job if you don't get them all off with a good cleaning. Also the high humidity present in most baths can deteriorate wallboard and plaster, so you need to inspect the surfaces carefully to make sure they're sound. I had done that.

On this job I was using a nonpasted wallpaper. "Good!" I thought. "That will let me use an extra-generous application of paste to make sure there's enough tack in the adhesive to keep the wallpaper where it's supposed to be—on the ceiling."

I slathered the paste on the back of the wallpaper, booked it properly, and started to install. I got only halfway across the ceiling with the first strip when the side I'd just installed started to peel. The only paper sticking to the ceiling was the part I was holding in my hands. Not a good sign.

Lesson learned: When applying wallpaper overhead, always put a layer of paste on the ceiling first and allow it to dry before applying the paste to the wallpaper and starting application. The dry adhesive will draw the moisture out of the wet adhesive and double the tack strength—making sure that what goes up doesn't come down.

RULES of Engagement

There are only two rules of engagement: 1) Maximize the width of the strips of material applied to the wall (wide strips adhere better); and 2) Minimize the number and length of seams (fewer seams mean fewer chances for lifted paper edges and pattern misalignments). Invoking these rules when working on your layout involves making a number of decisions and compromises. Here are some typical choices you may face. Try to end up with more good choices than bad ones.

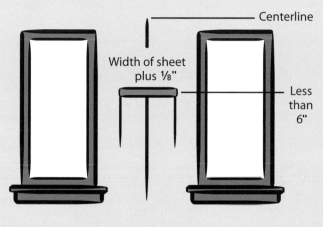

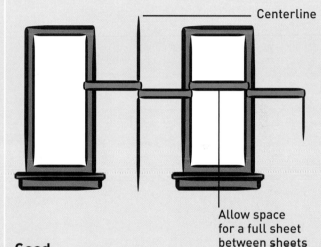

Bad

Centering a sheet of wallpaper between the windows results in two narrow strips of wallpaper adjoining the windows and two seams running the full height of the wall between the windows—the worst choice on two counts.

Good

This choice reduces the number of full-height seams between the windows to one and results in two wide sheets instead of one wide and two narrow—a better option.

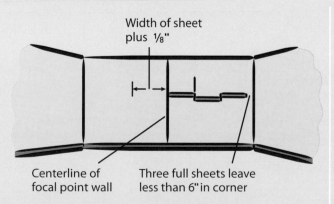

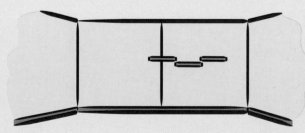

Bad

Aligning the edge of a sheet with the centerline of the focal point wall here leaves a narrow strip of wallpaper in the corner.

Good

Centering a sheet on the centerline of the focal point wall allows for a wider strip in the corner.

My Mistake

WHICH END IS UP?

Whether you're installing a border or an entire wall, take time to study the pattern before you start installation.

I was installing a beautiful and highly elaborate floral wallpaper early in my career. I was most of the way through the job before I noticed I'd hung the pattern upside down.

It was an expensive mistake because, although I still had some paper left over, I couldn't get the same dye lot when I went back to the supplier, so I had to buy a whole room's worth of paper and throw out the unused bolts from my earlier purchase.

It's a mistake that's easier to make than you might think, especially with somewhat abstract florals. Here's how to tell which end is up: Highlights are always on top; shadows are always beneath. Remember that much and you'll never have to stand on your head to admire your latest wallpapering job!

Lesson learned: The devil is in the details, and if you don't pay attention in the beginning of the job, he'll burn you in the end.

The first principle says to begin the first trial layout at the center of the room's focal point wall. The focal point wall is the one your eye is naturally drawn to when you enter the room. That's generally one of these spots:

● The portion of wall above a fireplace.

● The largest section of exposed wall in a bathroom or kitchen.

● The main section of wall in a kitchen eating area.

● The first wall you see as you enter the room. The centerline runs down its middle (see below).

● The wall with the room's main window or windows (often located opposite the door). If there is only one window, no matter what its size, it becomes the focal point, and the centerline runs down its center. If there is more than one window but they are on different walls, the larger window is the focal point. If there are two or more windows close together or side by side, the focal point centerline lies midway between them (see below). If you have corner windows or windows near the corner on two adjoining walls, they make a focal corner. Your layout starts at the vertical centerline of this wall. Once you identify the focal point of the room, use a no. 1 pencil to lightly mark the centerline at eye level. This becomes the starting point for planning a trial layout of sheet positions.

Focal points in a room

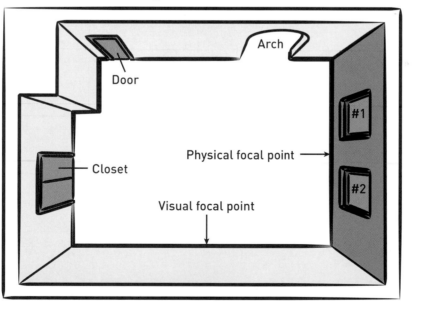

Arch

Door

#1

Closet

Physical focal point →

#2

Visual focal point

tips 'n' tricks

The starting point of your layout is not the point where you will start applying the wallpaper. That's an essential distinction: Planning the installation and doing the installation are two different processes, and they start at two different locations in the room. Deciding where to start applying wallpaper will be done later. For now just realize that the two starting points are going to be different.

My Mistake

WHEN IN A HURRY, SLOW DOWN

I was hanging wallpaper in a bathroom many years ago. There was a big dent in the drywall where someone had thrown the door open too hard one too many times and the knob had mashed into the wall.

I was young and in a hurry, so I used some so-called hot mud—drywall compound that's formulated to set up quickly so you don't have to wait overnight for it to dry.

Set up quickly it did. As soon as it felt firm to the touch, I papered right over it with a nice, shiny vinyl-coated paper with a foil finish to it. At first it looked great—no more dent, great-looking wallpaper. But when I came back into the room the next day after working elsewhere in the house, I discovered an ugly surprise. Not only had the dent partially reappeared, but also the wallpaper had discolored where I'd applied the compound. I had to cut out the whole section, repair it the slow, old-fashioned way, and install a patch. Hardly timesaving.

Lesson learned: Follow the package directions when using surfacing or drywall compound. Put on several thin coats rather than trying to fill a big dent with one application. If you don't, the surface of the patch will feel dry, but the material is still wet underneath. While drying, it can give off chemicals that stain the paper—and shrink in the process, making the smooth-as-glass repair magically disappear.

Creating a TRIAL LAYOUT

Once you've determined your focal-point wall, you can create a trial layout that determines where each sheet of wallpaper will go. Here's how:

1. Center the first sheet over the centerline of your focal point or align one edge with the centerline, whichever works best under the Rules of Engagement on page 189. Then measure and mark the seams lightly with a pencil for the rest of the room, adding ⅛ inch on average to allow for expansion when the paper is wet. Work from the corners of the focal-point wall to the dead corner.

2. Working from left to right, begin numbering the spaces between the marked seams in the order in which they will be hung. The first full-height strip will be sheet 1. This master sheet is the first you will hang, and it is the master pattern to which all other sheets will be matched.

3. Working from left to right, continue numbering the sheet positions around the room to the dead corner (2, 3, and so on) lightly in pencil. When you come to wide windows or other openings where you will split a sheet in two, label the upper section A and the bottom section B. Recessed windows or similar openings require duplicate sheets (step 6). Mark these sheets D. Number the sheets between the dead corner and the edge of the first sheet of wallpaper with negative numbers; those sheets will be hung from right to left instead of from left to right.

4. Once you have numbered each sheet location on the wall, measure the actual height of the wall in each slot in sequence, then add 4 inches.

tips 'n' tricks

"Height plus 4. Height plus 4. You can't go wrong with height plus 4." I make those who attend my wallpapering seminars chant these words until they're seared into their brains. That's because one of the easiest mistakes to make when installing wallpaper is to cut a sheet too short. Walls are rarely perfectly square, especially in older homes, and over the length of a room a slight angle to the ceiling or floor adds up. If you add 4 inches extra of selvage—2 inches at the top and 2 at the bottom—you'll have enough extra to cover for all but the most wacky, out-of-square rooms. So I repeat: The length measurement for each sheet that you enter on your layout chart is the height of the wall plus 4 inches, in every case.

5. Make a two-column chart on a piece of paper. Each horizontal line on the paper represents a sheet of wallpaper. In the left-hand column list each sheet number, starting with the lowest number (likely a negative number). In the right-hand column, write the length of each sheet. This layout chart is the blueprint that will guide you throughout installation. It tells you how many sheets you need, what the length of each sheet is, in what order the sheets will be applied to the wall, and exactly where each sheet will be placed.

6. Recessed windows (those without jamb casing) will not only require an A sheet above the window (long enough to cover the recess above the window) and a B sheet beneath the window (long enough to cover the sill below the window), but two D sheets, one duplicating the sheet coming into the window to cover the left recess and another duplicating the sheet coming out of the window to cover the right recess, as shown on page 197. For more on recessed windows, see pages 221–224.

Room layout

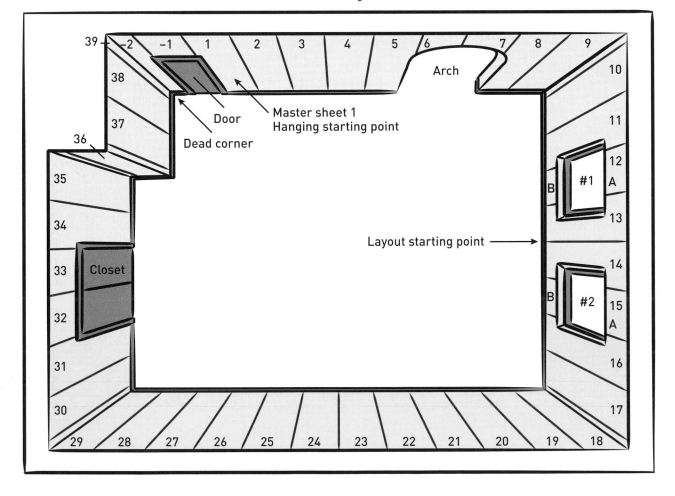

PLOTTING the Layout

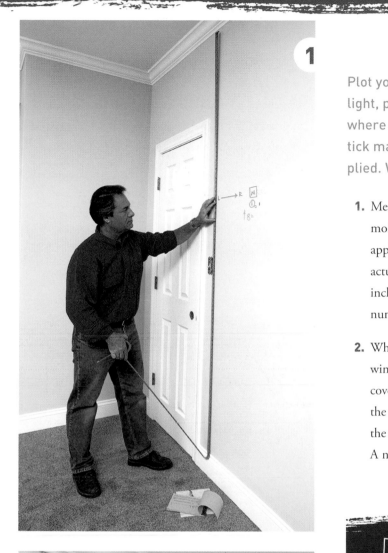

Plot your chosen layout onto the wall. First put light, penciled tick marks on the wall to mark where the seams fall. The spaces between the tick marks show where the sheets will be applied. We call these spaces *slots.*

1. Measure the room from the top of the baseboard molding to the bottom of the crown molding (if applicable) at each slot location. Add 4 inches to the actual measurement and note the resulting number of inches on your layout notepad next to the sheet number.

2. When you reach an interruption in the wall, such as a window, measure the amount of material required to cover the wall over the window plus the recess above the window. Add 4 inches to this amount and record the resulting number of inches on your notepad. Write A next to this sheet number.

tips 'n' tricks

Take a small, full-width piece of wallpaper to use as a template to help you visualize your layout. Unlike a stiff metal tape measure blade, the piece of wallpaper will wrap tightly around corners, giving you a more accurate sense of where the material's seams will actually fall.

tips 'n' tricks

You need to cut duplicate sheets in slots on either side of recessed windows and arches. Why? Because after you apply the sheets on either side of the window and the A and B sheets above and below the window, there will be two blank spots where there is no wallpaper at the top right and left of the window recess. You need two duplicate sheets to cover these patches: one that matches the pattern of the sheet on one side of the window, and one that matches the pattern of the sheet on the other side of the window. Both of these duplicate sheets are cut to the same length as the A sheet above the window. So for every recessed window you encounter, add a D sheet to your layout chart after the sheet for the slot before the window and a second D sheet to the layout chart after the sheet following the window (see the next page).

So your layout sheet should look like this:

11
11D
12A
12B
13
13D

3. Now measure the distance from the top of the baseboard molding to the bottom of the window molding. Add 4 inches to this amount and record the resulting number of inches on your notepad. Write B next to this sheet number. The number will be the same as the number of the sheet above the window because the sheet is within the same slot. Only the letter will be different.

Create a BLUEPRINT for Success

Once you've made several trial layouts and selected the one that works best in your room, you can commit the plan to paper. That means working your way around the room, noting the measurements of each slot that will receive a *drop* of wallpaper. Write down the sequential order of the slots, working from left to right, and the drop length required for each drop to cover all the walls properly on your written layout, as shown at right.

Create your written layout on a lined 5×7 notepad—a handy size to carry around. Each line represents one sheet. The left-hand column shows the sheet number, starting with the lowest number on your layout. (Negative slots are those to the left of the master sheet. There is no zero.) To the right of the sheet number and on the same line, write the length of the sheet. The length is equal to the height of the wall the sheet is to cover plus 4 inches. On the next line, write the number and length of the next sheet, and so on around the room.

Remember that recessed windows will require an A sheet above the window and a B sheet beneath the window, and also two D sheets, one duplicating the sheet coming into the window and the other duplicating the sheet coming out of the window, as shown below.

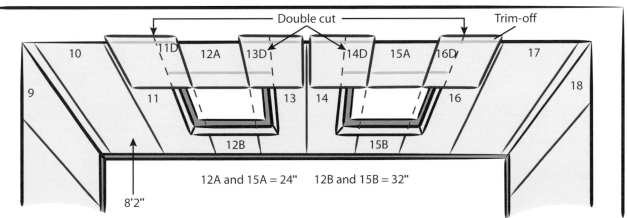

Window layout

Double cut   Trim-off

10   11D   12A   13D   14D   15A   16D   17

9   11   13   14   16   18

12B   15B

12A and 15A = 24"   12B and 15B = 32"

8'2"

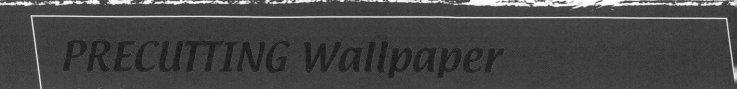

PRECUTTING Wallpaper

Wallpaper is a lot easier to deal with dry and flat than it is wet and vertical. So while the wallpaper is still dry, I precut bolts into sheets 4 inches longer than the wall to which they'll be applied. That way, when it is time to apply them, they're already of manageable length and require only a slight trim once they're hung on the wall. Still, it surprises me how many people—including many professional wallpapering contractors—wrestle with long sheets of sticky, slimy wallpaper. Don't be one of these people; precut and organize your material first. The job will go much faster, and a quality result will be much easier to achieve.

wizard WARNING

Here's where teamwork is especially important: helping one another ensure that the material is cut properly. It takes two to handle and position large sheets of material, and two sets of eyes are important to double-check that the material is cut to the right length and numbered correctly.

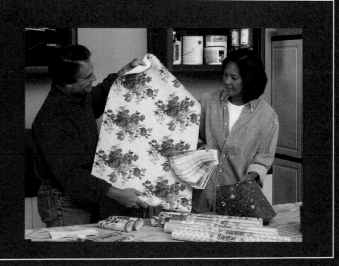

WRONG WAY: The cut bisects the key element.

RIGHT WAY: The cut leaves 2 inches clearance above the key element.

Straight match

With a straight match, the master sheet is the sheet you hang first and the visual reference used to cut the rest of the sheets. Its length is the height of the wall plus 4 inches. Before cutting the master sheet, determine the key element in the wallpaper pattern. To identify the key element, blur your focus a bit as you look at the pattern and identify the strongest element you see. It repeats throughout the sheet. (The large red rose is the key element in the pattern shown here.) Avoid cutting through the key element at the top of the wall. To ensure that the entire element appears at the top of the wall, leave at least 2 inches of pattern showing above the key element, plus another 2 inches for selvage.

1. Once you've cut the master sheet, leave it on the table. Then unroll the second sheet on top of the master sheet.

2. Check the left-hand edge of the master sheet against the right-hand edge of the material you've just unrolled. If the same element is in the same place on both sheets, your wallpaper material is a straight match.

3. Match the left edge of the material you've just unrolled to the left edge of the master sheet and cut the unrolled sheet to the length shown on your layout chart. The A sheets are measured from the top of the master sheet.

4. Cut all subsequent sheets in the same manner. Stack them directly on top of the second sheet you cut. Offset that stack slightly from the master sheet, leaving about 1 inch of master sheet showing to make sure you're matching the pattern with each cut you make. Number the sheets lightly on the back in the upper left-hand corner using a no. 1 pencil. Check the numbers periodically to make sure you haven't skipped a sheet.

5. Measure up from the bottom of the sheet when cutting the sheets designated with a letter B. To avoid damaging the sheets underneath, cut the material by laying a carpenter's square across the paper at the cut point. Lift the paper along the edge of the square, tearing it neatly.

6. An alternate cutting method is to run a snap-blade knife along the carpenter's square. This method should be used only when cutting full sheets, when you are cutting directly on the tabletop, with no sheets underneath.

7. Remember to number each sheet after each cut. Once you have a neat stack of cut sheets on your table that correspond to the numbers of the sheets on your layout chart, you're ready to backroll the paper. Skip ahead to page 206.

Drop match

Drop match patterns are cut in a different way than straight match patterns: There are two master sheets—odd and even. That's because the paper's design is spread over the width of two sheets.

1. Unroll the material on the table, determine what its key element is, and decide where to cut the paper, as with a straight match. In this case a border will be installed at the top of this wallpaper, so you must factor in the width of the border plus 2 inches of selvage to determine where to cut. That's so the border won't run right over the pattern's key element.

2. Check the pattern match on the right-hand side. The key element should drop by half the repeat on the right-hand side of the sheet. Double-check to ensure that it does, so you know that you are, in fact, working with a drop match. With a drop match, even-numbered slots will match one master sheet, and odd-numbered slots will match another.

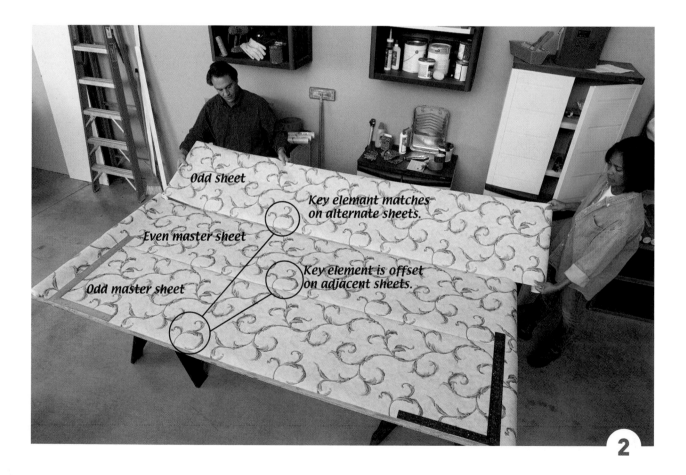

Odd sheet

Key elemant matches on alternate sheets.

Even master sheet

Key element is offset on adjacent sheets.

Odd master sheet

2

3. When applying a frieze at the top of the wall, allow for the 2-inch selvage at the top of the sheet, here represented by the 2-inch-wide carpenter's square, and the width of the border above the key element before precutting the sheet. That ensures that the border won't run on top of the key element. Cut the first (odd) master sheet. Then match the drop pattern on the next sheet and cut it to length for the even master sheet.

4. To make sure you always match odd-numbered sheets to your odd-sheet master and even sheets to your even-sheet master, make a notation column directly on the table as I have in the photo. Odd sheets are designated O; evens are designated E; S stands for *stack.* Match all successive odds and evens to the two original master sheets, then put the successive sheets on the stack. Sheets 1, 3, and 5 have the key element in one position (under the pink knife), and sheets 2 and 4 have the key element in another position (under the orange knife). If you continually match odd sheets to the no. 1 master sheet and even sheets to the no. 2 master sheet, you cannot make a mistake and miscut. Cutting wallpaper by tearing it against a carpenter's square allows you to make a straight, square cut, and the square's weight keeps the paper from curling.

how a drop match pattern works

The snap-blade knives in this photo show where the key element is at either side of each sheet. Note that the key element drops by half the distance of the repeat from one side of each sheet to the other.

Random match

Because there is no repeating horizontal pattern in random match patterns, you can cut sheets continuously off the roll. Random match wallpaper is reverse-hung: The bottom of every other sheet is placed near the ceiling. That's because sometimes printing presses print one side of a sheet darker than the other. Reverse-hanging butts like sides against one another, preventing sharp changes in shade that would manifest as vertical bands if the sheets were hung with unlike sides butting. Keep track of the material's orientation by sketching a small arrow on the wall after the sheet number: an up arrow for sheet 1, a down arrow for sheet 2, and so on. Number the tops of each sheet when cutting, as for other types of patterns.

Mark sheet number in corner

tips 'n' tricks

Natural materials such as grass cloth have no large, repeating pattern, so you can simply roll them out and cut the pieces to length. For that reason there's very little waste when applying these materials. That's a good thing because natural materials are usually fairly expensive.

Measure master sheet

Cut sheets to master

My Mistake

KEEP YOUR EYE ON THE DYE!

Numbers matter. Before opening a single package of wallpaper, check the dye lot and pattern numbers on the wallpaper itself. One digit off can make the difference between a great job and an unacceptable one.

When I was just an apprentice wallpaper installer, I worked for my grandfather. One of the first rooms I worked on required about 14 bolts of wallpaper. To save time (and you'll see the irony of that later), I read only the first four digits of the numbers on each bolt. They all matched, and I assumed the rest of the digits did too.

That was a bad assumption. When I finished the job and stood back to look at it, the room looked terrible. It turns out the numbers I had read were the pattern numbers, and yes, the pattern on all sheets was identical. But the last three digits—the ones I didn't read—were the dye lot. And it turns out I had bolts that came from four different dye lots. That meant every fourth sheet or so changed color slightly. And since this particular pattern was a dark, saturated color, you really noticed it. Your eye always goes to what's different, not what's the same. On this room's big, flat, open walls, the effect was dreadful.

Lesson learned: I had to do the whole job over again—but I never again hung a single sheet of wallpaper without ensuring that the numbers matched—all of them.

PROCESSING Wallpaper

After the wallpaper is cut, labeled, and laid on the worktable, it's ready for processing. Process the paper in two steps.

Backrolling

Roll each individual sheet from the bottom up so that the pattern is on the inside and the number on the back of the sheet is visible. Secure the roll with a no. 10 rubber band. Backrolling takes the twist out of the wallpaper sheet so that it will lie flat as it comes out of the water tray and exposes the prepasted side, allowing water to activate the paste. The number on the back of the sheet is easy to see, helping you to keep the sheets in the order you will apply them to the wall. The cylinders are easier to handle than sheets for the next steps.

Sequencing

The last piece of paper you cut will be the highest numbered drop. Usually it's the one that will be hung in the dead corner. Start the backrolling process with this sheet. Roll that sheet and secure it with a rubber band, then place it on the table beside you. It will form the first roll in a neat stack that you will build on the table. Continue to roll each succeeding sheet in descending numerical order, placing them side by side in order, until you have an array of rolls that is square. Continue rolling, stacking the next course of rolls at a 90-degree angle to the first. This keeps the stack stable. Continue in this manner until you have rolled all the sheets. Finally, backroll your borders and place them on top of the stack.

ACTIVATING and BOOKING

Booking allows you to work with a neat package of material rather than a long, unwieldy sheet. Before installing the wallpaper, you must activate prepasted wallpaper or apply adhesive to nonpasted paper. An important part of this operation is booking (folding) the wallpaper. Booking keeps the paste from drying out and prevents debris from contaminating the adhesive. It allows moisture to soak fully and evenly into the backing to promote better adhesion. Proper booking allows the wallpaper to expand evenly. It also makes the wallpaper easier to handle during installation. To speed up the job, one person can activate (or apply paste) and book the wallpaper while another installs it.

Prepasted wallpaper

1. Fill a plastic garden planter box or water tray three-fourths full of water at 72 to 80 degrees. Warmer water will harm the adhesive and overexpand the paper; cooler water won't activate the adhesive. Remove the rubber band and loosen the first sheet so water can get between the layers. Soak the sheet in the water according to the manufacturer's instructions, timing it carefully. Oversoaking dissolves adhesive; undersoaking doesn't activate the adhesive.

tips 'n' tricks

To better control the penetration of the water into the wallpaper adhesive, add some common household chemicals to your activating solution. For hard water, add ⅛ teaspoon water softener to 1 gallon water. For soft water, add a capful of ammonia or 1 teaspoon table salt to 1 gallon water. In the cases of all additives, don't exceed these amounts: More is not better. These additives have the effect of making the water wetter and better able to penetrate and activate the wallpaper adhesive.

2. Grab each corner of one end of the strip and slowly pull three-fourths of its length from the water tray, paste side up. Check the back for uniform wetness and splash any dry spots with water from the tray. Fold the top edge of the strip to the middle of the sheet, the pasted faces together. Align the edges, or seams, and smooth but do not crease the fold.

3. Slowly pull out the rest of the sheet. Check it for wetness and wet dry spots as necessary. Fold the bottom up and tuck it under the top edge so the ends overlap about 1 inch. This keeps the ends and middle of the sheet from drying out. Align and smooth as you did the top section.

4. To book the wallpaper, fold the farthest fold to the fold nearest the water tray and repeat. The sheet is now booked. Activate and book five more strips to make a stack of six. Stack the booked sheets on a towel on the floor beside the worktable. Repeat for all sheets, working in sequence. Let activated sheets sit 5 to 15 minutes.

5. When you have booked a stack of about six sheets, flip the wet stack over and slide it into a plastic kitchen trash bag and close it with a twist tie to keep the air out and the moisture in. Now the sheets are in sequence and ready to apply to the wall. Sheets can remain in the bag until you're ready to apply that stack to the wall—a minimum of five minutes and a maximum of three hours. Leaving the wallpaper bagged any longer than three hours risks creasing the material. Write the sheet numbers on the outside of each bag and distribute the bags around the room near the walls to which the sheets will be applied.

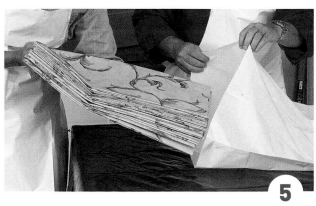

Nonpasted wallpaper

Nonpasted wallpaper cannot be immersed in water because the materials are delicate and likely to stain. Some organic materials could disintegrate if immersed. Because of this, adhesive is applied in two steps to allow the paper to absorb the moisture necessary for good adhesion. Clear, ready-mix vinyl adhesive is the best choice of adhesive: It bonds well, is unlikely to stain, and is washable, so if it does get on something you can wipe it off.

There are two categories of nonpasted paper: vinyls and naturals. Vinyls have a vinyl surface and a paper backing. These are laid out, precut, backrolled, and sequenced in exactly the same way as prepasted wallpapers. For this type of material, unroll and apply adhesive to the back one sheet at a time. Naturals, on the other hand, are precut, numbered, and rolled continuously from bottom to top. When you're ready to apply adhesive to naturals, simply unroll the entire stack with the natural side down and the backing side up on your worktable. Apply adhesive to the sheets one at a time, removing each sheet from the stack after you have applied paste to it.

quiz the WIZ

Should I paste prepasted wallpaper?

Absolutely not! Adhesives applied at the factory are carefully matched to the backing material. Adhesives have come a long way in the past few decades. Early prepasted wallpapers didn't always adhere well, so some installers routinely applied a second layer of paste manually. That's no longer necessary and, in fact, can cause problems: The adhesive you apply may not be compatible with the factory-applied adhesive or the material backing itself. Prepasted paper needs to be activated with 100 percent water. When you use an adhesive, the material ends up water-starved and can stick to itself during the booking process, destroying the paper. If you're applying wallpaper to a ceiling or high-moisture area, or if you're the belt-and-suspenders type who wants extra assurance that your wallpaper will stick, apply the paste to the wall—not the wallpaper—and allow it to dry. Then activate, book, and apply the prepasted wallpaper according to instructions. The dried adhesive on the wall will pull moisture from the adhesive on the wallpaper and result in an even stronger bond.

cool tools

Stack buckets to put your paste tray and water bucket at table height so you don't have to bend over to access them. And here's another Wizard trick: Slide the stack's two bottom sheets out—one toward one side of the table, one toward the other. They act as drop cloths, allowing you to paste beyond the edge of each sheet without getting adhesive on the table.

Ready your application table by assembling a regular paint roller cover, a roller tray, a bucket of clean water and a large sponge, and drying towels. Load the adhesive onto the roller as you would paint. Make a long stroke down the middle of the sheet and one down each seam of the material. We call this the *dump.* The next step, called the *set,* uses a W or an M pattern to spread the adhesive evenly over the entire back of the sheet, as shown below. The final step, called the *lay,* rolls the adhesive the full length of the sheet in parallel strokes to ensure an even coating over the length of the sheet. Cover the sheet in the three steps, then go through the three steps again. This ensures that there's enough moisture in the paper to prevent it from drying and sticking to itself during the booking process; it also ensures that there's enough adhesive to bond the sheet securely to the wall. Double-pasting is a smart move: It takes only an extra couple minutes per sheet, but it is great insurance against poor adhesion.

After pasting, book each sheet the same way you would prepasted wallpapers after activation. Install booked natural sheets within two to three minutes to ensure that the adhesive doesn't begin to dry before the material is installed. Unlike vinyls, which absorb water only in their backing, naturals absorb moisture into the entire material and can dry out much faster than vinyls can. Book and bag two or three sheets of vinyl at a time. Keep a clean surface—if adhesive gets onto the table, clean it off with the sponge and water and dry it with a towel immediately so it won't transfer to the face of the material.

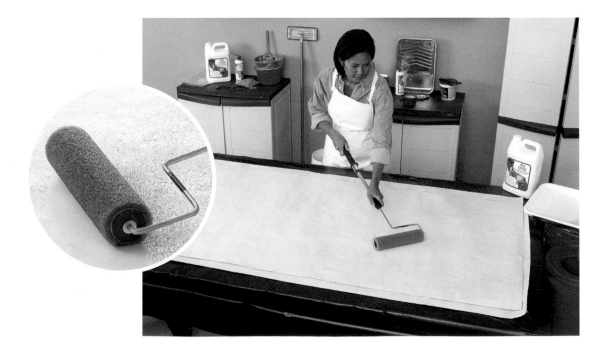

HANG IT

A sheet of wallpaper changes its name and becomes a drop when you hang it on a wall. A sheet is dry and horizontal; a drop is wet and vertical.

Wallpaper is easier to install and adheres better if you handle it gently. Don't push, pull, shove, or press it in place to get a good seal; rough handling stretches the material and pushes the adhesive out of place, causing wavy seams that are more visible and corners that are more likely to pull away from the wall after they dry. Wallpaper dries in three to five days.

Every numbered drop of wallpaper goes on the wall in the same way. Place the ladder directly in front of the space where the first drop will go. Put the 4-inch broad knife, smoothing brush, and snap-off-tip knives in your apron or tool pouch pockets. Hang the first drop, then additional drops in sequence, following these steps:

1. Snap a plumb chalkline to mark the right edge of the first drop (top left photo). Climb the ladder and unfold the top portion of the booked drop. The weight of the folded bottom holds the drop straight while you work with the top half. Align the edge of the drop with the line. Let a 2-inch selvage overlap the ceiling. Position the key element 2 inches below the top of the wall.

2. Tap the drop into the ceiling line with the wallpapering brush and crease it into the corner with a broad knife so the 2-inch margin flaps onto the ceiling or molding. Then smooth the material on the wall with downward strokes of the brush.

3. Climb down and move the ladder out of the way. Open the bottom half of the drop and smooth it against the wall with the brush. Crease the wallpaper into the base molding so the 2-inch margin overlaps the baseboard. Trim the bottom, guiding the knife with the broad knife. As you trim, slide the broad knife along the cut without lifting the cutting knife tip from the wallpaper.

4. Using the broad knife as a guide, trim off the excess paper at the ceiling with a cutting knife. Start with a new snap-off knife tip for each cut.

5. Gently lift the edge and wipe away the chalkline. Smooth the edge back into place with the brush. Then brush the entire sheet one more time. If some bubbles won't work out, don't worry about them now. Most will disappear as the wallpaper shrinks when drying. The goal is to eliminate air, not adhesive. Continue hanging drops around the room.

6. After installing two or three drops, wash the wall and molding with clear water and a sponge to remove adhesive residue. Wash from the top down. Dry the wall with a towel to reduce waterspotting. If you have a helper, the helper can wash while you continue installing drops.

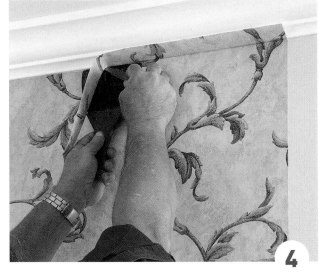

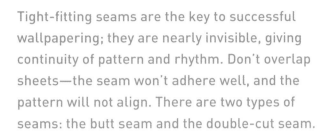
Seams

Tight-fitting seams are the key to successful wallpapering; they are nearly invisible, giving continuity of pattern and rhythm. Don't overlap sheets—the seam won't adhere well, and the pattern will not align. There are two types of seams: the butt seam and the double-cut seam.

The **butt seam** is the most common wallpaper seam. The sheets butt snugly against one another, edge to edge. Don't put too much pressure on the seam as you smooth it down or you'll stretch the material out of square—and your seam will no longer be vertical. Even a tiny amount of stretch per sheet can be a problem, as the distortion compounds with each abutting sheet until it can create a very visible mismatch—the sense that your walls are leaning. Or the material will shrink as it dries, leaving gaps instead of tight seams. So

brush seams gently and always vertically, never horizontally. Remember: When it comes to wallpaper, length is strength.

The **double-cut seam** is used for special situations, such as outside corners and borders. This seam starts with overlapping sheets. Using a carpenter's square or a straightedge as a guide, cut through both layers with the knife. Make the cut from the ceiling to the baseboard without cutting into the wall. Throw away the scrap from the sheet on top. Then carefully lift the edge of the top sheet and pull out the trimmed scrap from the sheet underneath. The two sheets will now butt together along the cut edges, and the pattern will match. Gently smooth the seam with your brush.

Setting a seam

To set a seam, brush it with a wallpaper smoothing brush to eliminate air. Gently tap the seam with the bristle edge of the brush to tighten the bond. Then lightly pull a plastic float up and down across the seam instead of rolling it—a seam roller squeezes out the adhesive. The float levels the seam without squeezing out the adhesive. Always work vertically; going horizontally across the seam will pull the wallpaper out of alignment.

Butt seam

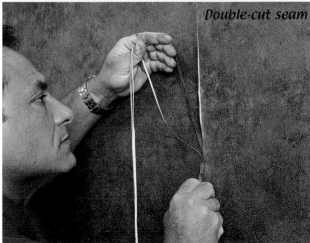

Double-cut seam

Good

Bad

My Mistake

DOINNGG! OVERSTRESSING A TOOL CAN LEAD TO DISASTER!

I was using a snap-blade knife to trim wallpaper. It's the kind with a razor edge and a sharp point. You don't need to change blades when this knife is dull—you simply press sideways on the blade's tip and it snaps cleanly off, making a new sharp tip ready to cut. When you've used the entire length of the blade, you simply discard the blade holder. It's a great tool, but it deserves respect, and it has its limitations.

Once I made the mistake of putting too much sideways pressure on the blade while I was cutting. Doinngg! The blade tip snapped off, flew up, and impaled itself in my cheek. I still have the scar. Had the tip landed an inch and a half from where it did, I might have lost sight in one eye.

Lesson learned: Don't over-stress your tools. And when you snap off an old blade, do it safely inside the pocket of a heavy leather work-apron pouch. The leather protects you from the sharp blade and the pouch keeps it from flying into the air—and retains all the used blades in one place so you can safely dispose of them when your job is done.

Trim the wallpaper into inside corners, such as at the ceiling joint, at wall corners, when meeting moldings, and in similar places. Some of the pattern is lost in trimming, so the pattern rarely matches in inside corners.

Cutting inside corners

When hanging the last sheet on a wall into a corner, split the paper into two separate pieces. This prevents the paper from buckling and wrinkling in the corner and keeps the pattern aligned vertically, though not always perfectly matched. Here's how to make the corner:

1. Install the left side of the wallpaper sheet on the wall coming into the corner. Let the right side overlap onto the other wall.

2. Crease the wallpaper into the corner. Using a 4-inch metal broad knife as a guide, slide your snap-blade knife down the inside of the corner to separate the two pieces. This method, called *scribing,* allows you to follow the slight imperfections of the corner as you cut, making them less noticeable to the eye.

3. Measure the width of the leftover piece. Subtract ¼ inch, then snap a plumb line on the new wall at this distance from the corner. Install the second sheet with its right edge against the plumb line. Overlap it onto the first sheet.

4. Double-cut the corner. The pattern won't match exactly in the corner, but your eye won't see the slight misalignment in an inside corner. What's much more important is to start with the first seam on the new wall absolutely plumb. By relieving a bit of misalignment in the corner, you prevent a larger mismatch on a butt seam in the middle of the wall. Also, houses settle over time, and walls may move independently of one another. If you don't cut the inside corner, the paper can pucker and wrinkle there.

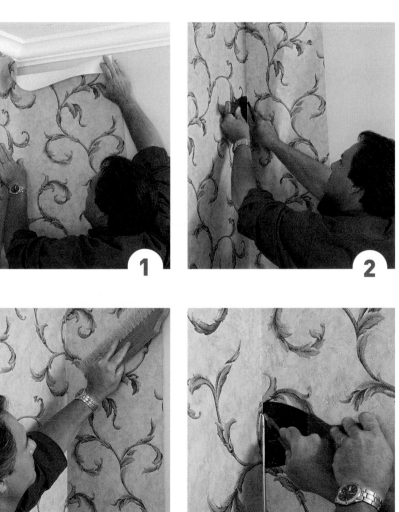

Wrapping outside corners

Wrap outside corners to prevent the wallpaper from lifting off the wall when someone or something brushes up against it. To realign the pattern to fit the plane of the new wall, strike a new plumb line on the new wall; you will realign the pattern at the seam following the outside corner. That means the pattern will not match perfectly here. But in the case of an outside corner, aligning the pattern at the seam following the corner offers the best compromise between durability and aesthetics. The sheet numbers in the steps refer to the room illustration on page 194.

1. Measure the width of your wallpaper sheet. Subtract ¼ inch. Then snap a plumb line that distance from the last seam before the outside corner (the right edge of sheet 36). Apply sheet 36 to the wall, butting the right edge against the plumb line on the new wall.

2. Make a small vertical cut through the trim-off at the top and bottom of the sheet where it rounds the corner. This will allow you to smooth the sheet to the wall without wrinkles.

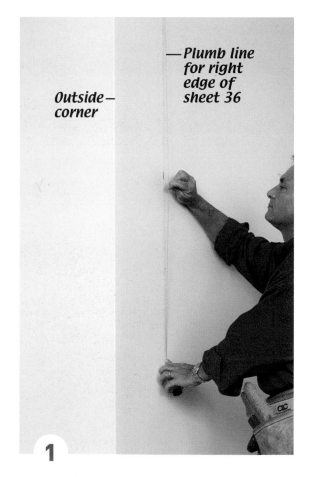

Outside— corner

—Plumb line for right edge of sheet 36

1

Sheet 36

2

3. Wrap sheet 36 around the corner, smoothing it onto the right-hand wall with gentle vertical strokes of your wallpaper brush. With the knife and long straightedge, make a double-cut seam where it overlaps sheet 35.

4. Remove the selvage from the top and bottom of the sheet by scribing and cutting to the ceiling or cove molding and baseboard using your 4-inch metal broad knife as a guide.

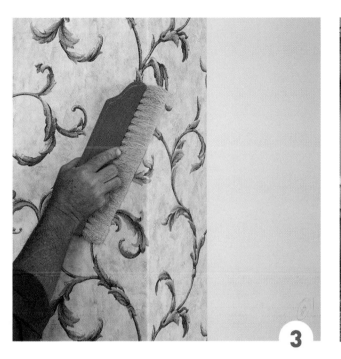

tips 'n' tricks

If you want to end the wallpaper at an outside corner, start by installing the wallpaper as if you were going to go around the corner but let the excess extend past the corner instead of smoothing it down. Hold the excess wallpaper taut with one hand and, holding your knife at a 45-degree angle. Cutting from the face side, make a sliding cut down the corner. This leaves a clean edge that won't fray or peel. If you want to give an outside corner in a high-traffic area some additional protection, install corner protectors. They're available in both soft, colored vinyl or hard, clear polycarbonate. Both types have a peel-and-stick adhesive and are easy to apply. I prefer the polycarbonate type myself—they really take a beating and are almost invisible.

Cutting Around TRIM

When cutting around trim, secure the sheet at the top with your wallpaper brush. Working down from the top, make a series of small cuts at 45-degree angles wherever the sheet comes in contact with a piece of molding. These incisions, called *tension cuts* or *relief cuts,* allow the flat paper to fit around the protrusion and lie flat against the wall. Here's how the procedure works:

1. Hang the drop, leaving the bottom half booked. Press the wallpaper against the trim molding with your smoothing brush. The paper should now hang over the opening.

2. If there is a large amount of wallpaper over the opening, cut away most of the excess at the top half of the opening to get it out of your way. Then cut from the top corner of the molding with scissors to the edge of the wallpaper at a 45-degree angle. Make a very small cut—perhaps just a ½-inch incision, such as the one I'm pointing to in the photo. A relief cut should always be done with a fresh blade to ensure a clean and precise cut.

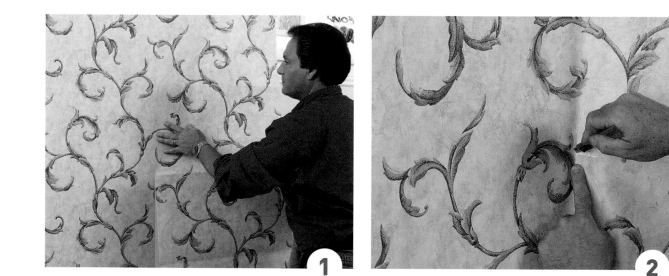

wizard WARNING

Eliminate waves or bubbles BEFORE you trim around moldings. Waves or bubbles will throw off your trim cut, creating either an overlap of the wallpaper onto the molding or, worse, a gap between the wallpaper and the molding. Wrinkles and bubbles are fairly common but fairly easy to deal with: Simply lift the sheet up and lay it down again, brushing it gently onto the wall. Once it's lying perfectly flat, make your trim cuts.

3. Hold the free edge of the sheet with one hand and make a sliding cut, using the molding as a guide. Stop your cut when you reach the small incision you made in step 2.

4. Use your metal broad knife to protect the sheet and act as a trim guide when making a scribing cut around the moldings.

This is where the time and effort you spent caulking around the trim really pays off—you'll get nice, smooth, precise cuts that are almost effortless to achieve and look great (see pages 74–75). Working from the top down allows you to keep the paper parallel to the wall while progressively relieving the tension caused by the molding protrusions as you work your way down the wall.

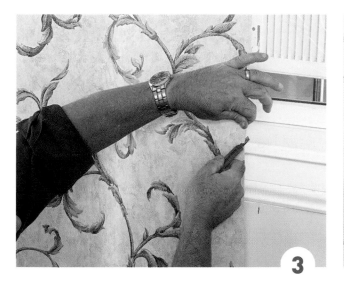

tips 'n' tricks

Don't be a cheapskate with snap-blade knives. Before you make each new cut, snap a new blade every single time. Wall materials dull blades fast, and you need a razor-sharp edge to get a precise cut. Knife tips are cheap. Wallpaper isn't. So cut, snap, cut, snap. I'll usually use one whole knife blade—that's 12 tips—for each sheet I hang. After the job, clean up the blade tips. I attach a magnet to a leather glove and go over the area and usually find a few small knife tips. You don't want to be pulling a blade out of the paw of your cat—or worse.

My Mistake

YIKES! KNOW WHEN TO LET NATURE TAKE ITS COURSE

When things start to go wrong, sometimes the best thing you can do is to let them. Attempting a heroic save can often do more harm than good.

I had just finished installing a strip of wallpaper in a kitchen with linoleum floors. More precisely, I had almost finished installing it—I'd dropped my snap-blade trimming knife, so I couldn't trim the top. I had just descended the ladder to retrieve the knife when I noticed that the loose paper at the top of the strip was heavy enough to overcome the bonding strength of the wallpaper adhesive. The whole strip was starting to peel off the wall. Stupidly I leaped forward to try to prevent the strip from peeling, knocking over the ladder. If that weren't bad enough, I leaped again to try to catch the ladder. My feet slipped, and I fell full-force into the ladder. The ladder punched a hole in the wall, and the wallpaper strip peeled off anyway, covering me with now-ruined paper and slimy adhesive. It was a true Three Stooges moment. It hurt too.

Another time my trimming knife slipped out of my hand and started to fall. I reached out and caught it in midair, closing my hand on the razor-sharp blade. My elation at that save, as you might imagine, was quite short-lived.

Lesson learned: Don't let your reflexes overcome your intelligence. If you drop a sharp knife, let it go. If something's falling on you, get out of the way. Reserve acrobatic saves for the tennis court, when the most you have to bruise is your ego.

RECESSED Windows and Doors

Wallpaper is two-dimensional. When wall features are recessed, though, wallpaper is taken into a three-dimensional space. That requires an additional technique: the duplicate method. This allows the pattern to match across the face of the wall and on the inside face of the window, and it allows the wrapping of all outside corners. The payoff is a beautifully maintained pattern and a durable, secure, long-lasting installation. That's particularly important around windows, where condensation and moisture can challenge wallpaper adhesion. Windows, doorways, wall niches, and other openings without moldings around them call for this treatment.

To wallpaper around a window, follow the same procedures as for other openings. You will need a duplicate sheet for the sheet at each side of the window. The pattern of the duplicate sheet matches the pattern on the top of the full-length sheet beside the window exactly but is the length of the A sheet that falls in the next slot.

1. Hang the sheet coming into the window, number 11 in the room shown on page 194, allowing the sheet to overlap the window opening. Set the seam.

2. Make a sliding cut along the top and the bottom of the window opening with your snap-blade knife. This frees the portion of the sheet overlapping the window opening to wrap into the window casing. Smooth the paper into the casing, then trim off excess material.

3. Apply the 12A sheet on the wall above the window.

4. Wrap the 12A sheet into the window casing and smooth down.

5. Apply the 12B sheet on the wall beneath the window.

6. Apply the next full sheet, number 13, coming out of the window. Make sliding cuts at the top and bottom of the window opening and wrap the material into the window casing as you did in step 2.

7. With your aluminum carpenter's square, place the short leg abutting the ceiling and the long leg 1 inch inside the window casing. Cut through the sheet and remove the excess material. Repeat on the other side of the window.

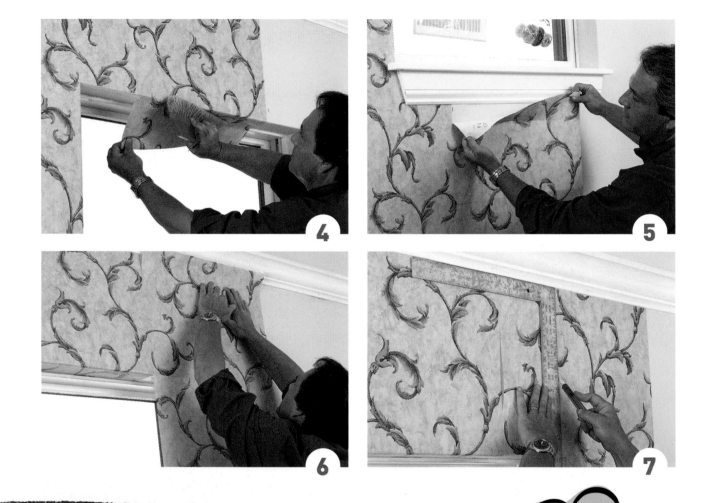

wizard WARNING

No matter how tempted you may be to pop a bubble in a drop, leave it alone. Adhesive generates bubbles through chemical action with water. As soon as the water content decreases through drying, the bubbles will go away. If there are wrinkles, immediately lift the drop and adjust it until it hangs straight.

8. Make a mark on each of the two duplicate sheets 1 inch wider than the distance from the edge of the A sheet to the corner of the window on either side.

9. Use your knife and carpenter's square to make a vertical cut at the mark you've made. This is called *splitting a sheet.*

10. Position—*slot in*—the two duplicates by matching the pattern to the A sheet.

11. Locate the corner of the window and carefully make a horizontal cut from the corner to the outside edge of the wallpaper. This small cut will allow the paper to wrap inside the window casing.

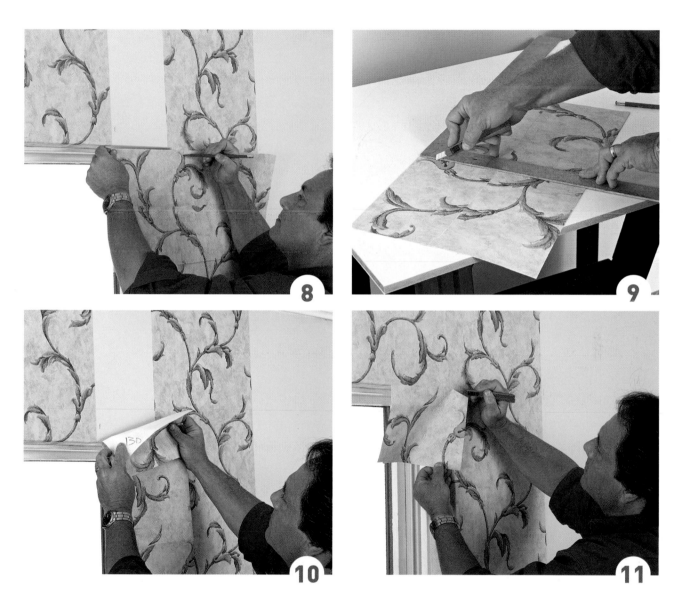

12. Trim off all excess inside the window. Notice that the pattern now matches, not only on the wall face but also inside the window casing. And this match wraps around the outside corner in accordance with the second law (cut inside corners; wrap outside corners). However this has broken the third law: Avoid overlaps. But this is a special overlap—it's an exact pattern match.

13. Place your carpenter's square with the short leg square to the ceiling and the long leg precisely aligned with the edge of the window. With a fresh tip of your snap-blade knife, slice through both layers of overlapped wallpaper with one smooth cut, using the edge of the square as a guide.

14. Reach underneath the seam created by this cut and remove the excess both under and over the seam. The result is a perfect double-cut matching seam.

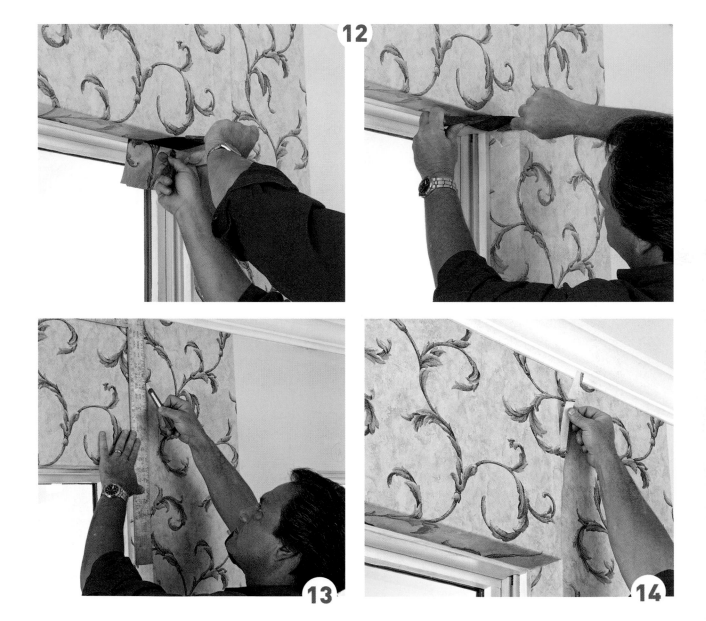

Repairing a GOUGE

If the worst happens—you tear the paper when you're moving furniture, or some similar mishap occurs—do you have to strip the whole wall and install new wallpaper? If you rely on this Wizard trick, it's almost as easy to repair damage as it is to cause it in the first place. Here's how to make a repair that's almost invisible:

1. The size of the gouge or tear doesn't matter—small or large, the technique for repairing it is the same. This technique also works for wallpaper that has been indelibly stained in a small area.

2. Find the area on a piece of leftover wallpaper that matches the pattern around the damaged area on the wall. Cut a patch from the leftover piece that extends at least 6 inches beyond the edge of the damaged area in all directions. Remove the torn flap.

3. Activate and book the patch you've just made. Carefully match the pattern on the wall to all edges of the patch. The pattern alignment must be perfect for this trick to work. If you misalign the pattern even slightly, your eye will go right to the imperfection. Take your time and get it right.

4. Lightly stroke the patch from the center outward in all directions with your float. Gently work the air out from beneath the patch but do not squeeze the adhesive out, stretch the material, or move the patch out of pattern alignment.

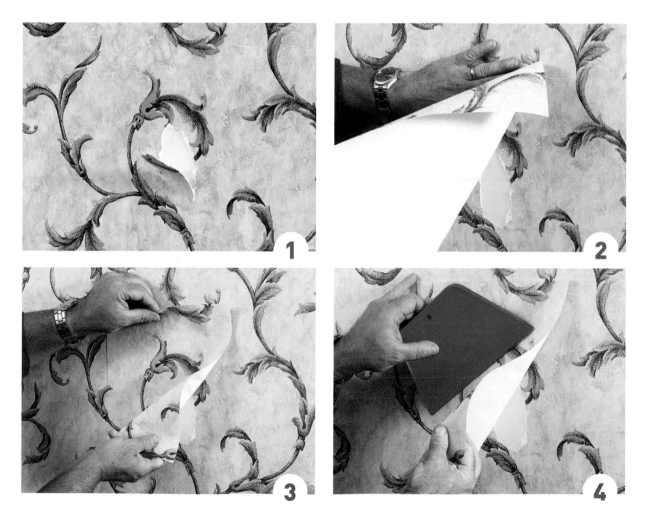

5. Using a snap-blade knife with a fresh tip, cut two intersecting crescent-shape cuts through the patch and the wallpaper beneath. This is called a *double-cut patch repair*. Cutting through the two identical layers with a single cut creates perfectly matched edges. Cut a football shape instead of a rectangle or triangle because your eye notices straight lines and multiple intersecting points more readily than curved lines. Keep the knife perpendicular to the wall.

6. You now have a duplicate piece of wallpaper that will replace the damaged piece. Remove the patch and book it again, folding paste side to paste side without creasing it. Put the patch in a resealable plastic bag. Then gently score or perforate the damaged piece inside the patch area. Mix a stripping solution of ½ cup fabric softener to 1 gallon water. Sponge this solution on the damaged area, cover the area with plastic wrap, and allow to sit for 20 to 30 minutes. The solution will break down the adhesive bond so you can lift off the damaged wallpaper. Do not damage the area beyond the patch or the cut edge, as that will ruin the effect. Remove remaining old adhesive from the area to be patched.

7. Remove the patch from the bag and smooth it into place with your float, carefully fitting it into the cutout area. Sponge down the area and let it dry.

tips 'n' tricks

If you have a roll and some scraps left over, wrap them in plastic wrap, place in a plastic trash bag, mark the bag with the name of the room it goes in along with the pattern and dye lot numbers, and store it in a cool, dry place. That way you have material you can use for a patch such as the one shown here.

Seams usually lift because of exposure to moisture or lack of adhesive. Repairing a seam calls for applying new adhesive to replace the old and re-expanding the material so that the seams will butt neatly. Here's how to fix a seam:

1. Pull back the sheets to the point where they are secure.

2. Mix four parts of seam repair adhesive or vinyl-to-vinyl adhesive with one part water.

3. Using a small brush, apply a thin, even coat of adhesive to the wall and backsides of the sheets. Leave the area open so that the water in the thinned adhesive will evaporate, causing the adhesive to get tacky. This usually takes three to five minutes.

4. Apply a second thin coat to the wall and the lifted edges of the sheets. Again allow the adhesive to get tacky. Adhesives will not work when they're wet; they work best when they're almost dry.

5. Gently tap the seams with the edge of the bristles of a wallpaper smoothing brush.

6. Pull a float lightly over the seam to level the edges of the paper to ensure even and adequate pressure to allow the adhesive to bond properly.

7. Wash off any adhesive residue so it will not stain the paper. Rinse with clean water and dry with a clean towel to eliminate the possibility of water spots.

seams easy

For small seam lifts, add 2 ounces of adhesive to 1 ounce water in a small container and stir. Gently lift the seam back to where it's secure. Wet the seam and wall with the solution using a small artist's brush. Wait three minutes or until the adhesive is tacky, then wet the surfaces again. When the second coat is tacky, gently set the seam with your float. Wash and dry.

Eliminating BUBBLES

Bubbles occur due to a chemical reaction—fermentation—that releases carbon dioxide as the adhesive dries. Bubbles are good because they tell you the adhesive process is working. But the vinyl surface can trap gas against the wall like a tent. Most bubbles will eventually flatten out as the wallpaper dries, which can take anywhere from two to five days. So don't overwork the material and displace the adhesive trying to eliminate bubbles while the material is still wet. Wait for the adhesive to cure, then see if the bubbles remain. If some still do, here's how to fix them:

For small bubbles

For bubbles between ½ inch and 3 inches in size, try this technique:

1. Mix four parts of seam repair adhesive with one part water.

2. Poke a small hole with a needle in the bottom of the bubble. This hole will allow the air in the bubble to escape as I fill it with adhesive. Later it will allow excess adhesive to escape as well. Load a meat marinating syringe—available at kitchen and gourmet stores—with the thinned adhesive. With the syringe parallel to the wall, gently insert the needle through the wallpaper into the top of the bubble. Do not penetrate the wall. Slowly inject thinned paste into the bubble. Don't completely fill the bubble, just inject enough to wet the wall and wallpaper surrounding the bubble. Otherwise, in fixing the bubble you may create a blister.

3. Carefully press the wallpaper back onto the wall with a float. Use three strokes: down to distribute the adhesive in the bubble, up to ensure complete distribution, and down again to force excess adhesive out the drain hole in the bottom of the bubble. Wash and dry the area thoroughly.

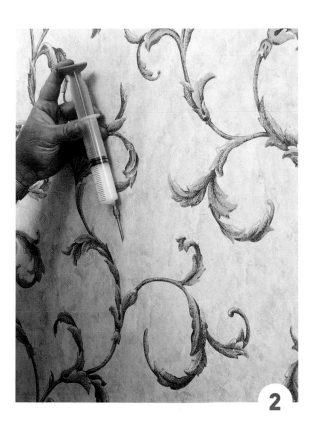

2

3

For large bubbles

1. Cut three-fourths of the way around the edge of the bubble, leaving the wallpaper attached at the top.

2. Gently lift the resulting flap and apply a thin coat of the seam repair adhesive solution to both the wall and the back of the paper. Leave the flap wet and open. Let the adhesive become tacky, then reapply a second thin coat.

3. After the second coat of adhesive becomes tacky, smooth the flap down onto the wall with a float. Gently rinse and dry the area.

appendix

Tool Checklists

On the pages that follow, you'll find handy checklists detailing the tools you need to tackle painting, faux finishing, and wallpapering jobs. Remember, the best tools meet four simple criteria:

- **Good quality.** Quality wears better, lasts longer, and produces better results.

- **Stainless steel or plastic.** Stainless steel or plastic are unaffected by paints, strippers, pastes, and solvents. They don't rust. Plus, they're easy to clean and long-lasting.

- **Brightly colored.** Fluorescent green, yellow, and orange tools are easy to spot in a work area.

- **Ergonomic.** Big, comfortable grips promote better tool control and reduce muscle fatigue and the risk of repetitive-strain injuries such as carpal tunnel syndrome.

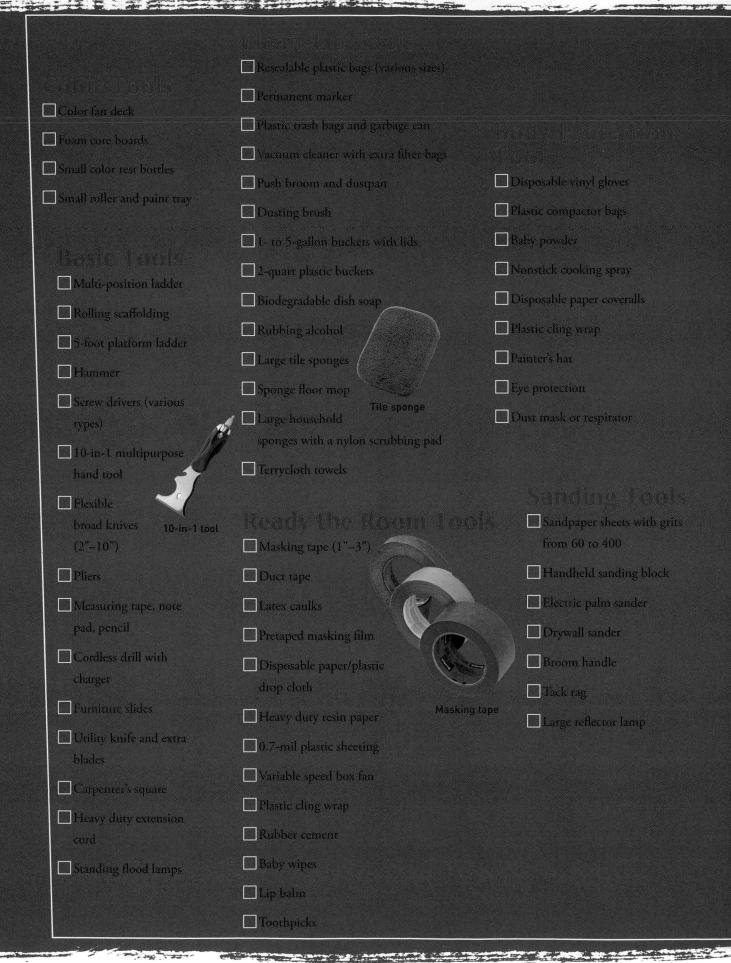

Color Tools

- [ ] Color fan deck
- [ ] Foam core boards
- [ ] Small color test bottles
- [ ] Small roller and paint tray

Basic Tools

- [ ] Multi-position ladder
- [ ] Rolling scaffolding
- [ ] 5-foot platform ladder
- [ ] Hammer
- [ ] Screw drivers (various types)
- [ ] 10-in-1 multipurpose hand tool
- [ ] Flexible broad knives (2"–10")
- [ ] Pliers
- [ ] Measuring tape, note pad, pencil
- [ ] Cordless drill with charger
- [ ] Furniture slides
- [ ] Utility knife and extra blades
- [ ] Carpenter's square
- [ ] Heavy duty extension cord
- [ ] Standing flood lamps

10-in-1 tool

Clean-Up Tools

- [ ] Resealable plastic bags (various sizes)
- [ ] Permanent marker
- [ ] Plastic trash bags and garbage can
- [ ] Vacuum cleaner with extra filter bags
- [ ] Push broom and dustpan
- [ ] Dusting brush
- [ ] 1- to 5-gallon buckets with lids
- [ ] 2-quart plastic buckets
- [ ] Biodegradable dish soap
- [ ] Rubbing alcohol
- [ ] Large tile sponges
- [ ] Sponge floor mop
- [ ] Large household sponges with a nylon scrubbing pad
- [ ] Terrycloth towels

Tile sponge

Ready the Room Tools

- [ ] Masking tape (1"–3")
- [ ] Duct tape
- [ ] Latex caulks
- [ ] Pretaped masking film
- [ ] Disposable paper/plastic drop cloth
- [ ] Heavy duty resin paper
- [ ] 0.7-mil plastic sheeting
- [ ] Variable speed box fan
- [ ] Plastic cling wrap
- [ ] Rubber cement
- [ ] Baby wipes
- [ ] Lip balm
- [ ] Toothpicks

Masking tape

Body Protection Tools

- [ ] Disposable vinyl gloves
- [ ] Plastic compactor bags
- [ ] Baby powder
- [ ] Nonstick cooking spray
- [ ] Disposable paper coveralls
- [ ] Plastic cling wrap
- [ ] Painter's hat
- [ ] Eye protection
- [ ] Dust mask or respirator

Sanding Tools

- [ ] Sandpaper sheets with grits from 60 to 400
- [ ] Handheld sanding block
- [ ] Electric palm sander
- [ ] Drywall sander
- [ ] Broom handle
- [ ] Tack rag
- [ ] Large reflector lamp

Wallpaper Removal Tools

- [ ] Closet dowel
- [ ] Snap-blade knives
- [ ] Plastic garden pump sprayer
- [ ] Perforation tool (Paper Tiger)
- [ ] Scraping tool (Paper Scraper)
- [ ] Baking soda
- [ ] Vinegar
- [ ] Liquid fabric softener
- [ ] Wallpaper remover concentrate
- [ ] 0.7-mil plastic sheeting
- [ ] Push pins
- [ ] Trigger-handle spray bottle
- [ ] Iodine

Faux Finishing Tools

- [ ] Small art brushes
- [ ] Truck tire brushes
- [ ] Window squeegee
- [ ] Fly swatter
- [ ] Plastic cling wrap
- [ ] Car duster mop
- [ ] Feather dusters
- [ ] Spring hair clips
- [ ] Plastic plates
- [ ] Latex paint conditioner
- [ ] Dish soap bottles
- [ ] 1-gallon plastic jug

Spring hair clip

Wall Repair Tools

- [ ] Replacement sheetrock
- [ ] Sheetrock screws
- [ ] Ring-shank sheetrock nails
- [ ] Wood strips
- [ ] Fiberglass mesh reinforcing tape
- [ ] Paper joint tape
- [ ] Mixing auger
- [ ] Quick-drying sheetrock compound
- [ ] Vinyl spackle
- [ ] Key hole sheetrock saw
- [ ] Oil-based sealer

Wallpapering Tools

- [ ] Leather tool pouch with belt
- [ ] Wallpaper smoothing brush
- [ ] Trimming broad knife
- [ ] Chalkline and push pins
- [ ] Plastic smoothing float
- [ ] Snap-blade knives with extra blades
- [ ] Aluminum framing squares
- [ ] Large plastic cutting board
- [ ] Scissors
- [ ] Rubber bands
- [ ] Spring hair clamps
- [ ] Activation tray
- [ ] Sponge roller cover
- [ ] Wallpaper adhesive
- [ ] Border applicator

Painting Tools

- [ ] Paint can opener and stir sticks
- [ ] Latex paint brushes (1"–3")
- [ ] Paint grate screen
- [ ] Oil-based paint brushes
- [ ] 2-quart paint bucket
- [ ] Metal roller tray with liners
- [ ] Extension poles
- [ ] Paint roller frame with various covers
- [ ] Hot-dog roller frame with various covers
- [ ] 4" paint pads
- [ ] Spray paint shield
- [ ] Electric spray painter

Roller frame and cover

Float

Disposal Tools

- [ ] Brush and roller spinner
- [ ] Resealable plastic bags (various sizes)
- [ ] Large glass jars with lids
- [ ] Mineral spirits
- [ ] Denatured alcohol
- [ ] Liquid fabric softener
- [ ] Cat litter

Index

NOTES